W9-AUL-117

The Anesthetic Society

Donald DeMarco

CHRISTENDOM PUBLICATIONS
Christendom College Press
Route 3, Box 87
Front Royal, Virginia 22630

L. C. Classification Number: CB430.D46
ISBN: 0-931888-09-3

NIHIL OBSTAT:
   Rev. Edward J. Berbusse, S.J., *Censor Librorum*
   September 30, 1982

IMPRIMATUR:
   †Most Rev. Thomas J. Welsh
   Bishop of Arlington
   October, 1982

For James Patrick:

The child we could

not embrace, has

embraced us.

The publication of this book was made possible in part through the support of the Christendom Publishing Group. Members are listed below:

Anonymous
Mr. & Mrs. John and Opal Baye
Mr. Joseph C. Berzanskis
Mr. John F. Bradley
Mr. George Bridgman
Mr. Joseph F. Brogan
Mrs. Martha Brown
Paul A. Busam, M.D.
Mr. Robert M. Caley
Mr. Charles M. Campbell
Miss Priscilla Carmody
Mr. Joseph C. Caserrelli, Esq.
Rev. Edward J. Connolly
Mr. John W. W. Cooper
Mr. Robert J. Cynkar
Mrs. Ellen L. Dalby
The Dateno Family
Rev. Herman J. Deimel
Mrs. George de Lorimier
Mr. Joseph L. DeStefano
Rev. Daniel B. Dixon
Mr. Francis Donahue
Mr. Thomas J. Dowdall
Mr. John H. Duffy
Rev. J. A. Duraczynski
Mrs. Clarence Ebert
Mr. D. N. Ehart
Mr. William W. Elliott
Rev. George S. Endal, S. J.
Mr. Francis G. Fanning
Mr. John F. Foell
Mr. J. P. Frank, Jr.
Mrs. Claudette Fredricksen
Mr. Richard L. Gerhards
Gysgt. R. P. Gideon
Mr. Patrick Guinan
Mr. Robert E. Hanna
Mrs. Mary J. Hart

Rev. Brian J. Hawker
Rev. Hugh P. Henneberry, S.S.J.
Arthur Hopkins, M.D.
Rev. John Horan
Mr. & Mrs. André Huck
Mrs. Doris L. Huff
Edgar Hull, M.D.
Rev. Jeffrey A. Ingham
Mr. Herman Jadloski
Mr. Edward E. Judge
Mr. & Mrs. Albert Kais
Rev. Michael J. Kelly
Mr. & Mrs. Frank Knoell
Mr. William C. Koneazny
James W. Lassiter, M.D.
Miss Thérèse Lawrence
Rev. Harry J. Lewis
Very Rev. Victor O. Lorenz
Mrs. Katherine I. MacDonald
Mr. George F. Manhardt
N. Anthony Mastropietro, M.D.
Mr. Thomas J. May
Rev. William R. McCarthy
Mr. John A. McCarty, Esq.
Mr. James McConnell
Mr. Robert McConville
Mr. Joseph D. McDaid
Mr. & Mrs. Dennis P. McEneany
Rev. P. J. McHugh
Mr. Thomas A. McLaughlin
Mr. J. R. McMahon
Mr. Robert Cruise McManus
Rev. Édward J. Melvin, C.M.
Mr. Larry Miggins
Rev. Hugh Monmonier
Mr. James B. Mooney (St. Gerard Foundation)
Col. Chester H. Morneau

(Continued on p. 182)

Let us go then, you and I,
When the evening is spread out against the sky
Like a patient etherised upon a table;

T. S. Eliot

Those are mentally ill who, stricken by a serious disease,
feel no pain.

Hippocrates

The greatest crimes are committed in the name of public
tranquility.

Tolstoy

Every mask and every pretense can be reduced to one
great evasion: the desire to overcome the sorrows of life
with palliatives and tricks of the imagination rather than
with sincerity and manly impulsion.

Ignazio Silone

In different versions, the chapters of this book first appeared in a variety of periodicals as follows:

1. Faith & Reason, *VIII, 3; Fall 1981*
2. Communio, *Summer 1980*
3. Homiletic & Pastoral Review, *April 1981*
4. Linacre Quarterly, *August 1978*
5. Child & Family Quarterly, *Vol. 14, No. 3*
6. Communio, *Fall 1980*
7. Fidelity, *I, 3; February 1982*
8. New Oxford Review, *October 1981*
9. Thought, *December 1981*
10. Homiletic & Pastoral Review, *July 1981*
11. Faith & Reason, *VI, 4; Winter 1980*
12. International Review of Natural Family Planning, *III, 3; Fall 1979*
13. Thought, *December 1980*

CONTENTS

Introduction

We refer to our mortal existence as 'life', although we know full well that all the while we live, we constantly experience death. Not death as such—what the coroner pronounces—but the smaller forms that are its intimations and prefigurements. We taste death in every disease, disability, and disappointment; in every distress, discouragement and disruption. Death invades our daily lives in every frustration of our will, in every momentary defeat, in every lost opportunity. Even in saying good-bye we sense the shadow of death. Death continuously plagues us and brings never ending conflict into our lives. Life is not merely life, therefore; it is a fine and mysterious weave of life and death.

Yet this is not necessarily a gloomy observation. On the contrary, because it is a realistic description of how we are fundamentally constituted, it is the only view of life that offers us any real hope. William Blake, whose familiar phrase—"fearful symmetry"—aptly describes the life-death tension of our human existence, reiterates the point when he writes:

> Man was made for joy and Woe;
> And when this we rightly know
> Thro' the world we safely go.[1]

When we accept life and death as being the very warp and woof of our existence, we accept conflict, but it is a conflict that is indispensable for heightened consciousness and moral growth. A life entirely devoid of conflict would be sterile, lacking any possibility for creative struggle. Like the newborn child who cries for its mother and in so doing develops its lungs, we need our own struggle to develop our strength.

Life with death, then, describes our human condition. Moreover, it specifies the elements of a dynamic opposition that provides us with

creative conflict. In T.S. Eliot's masterpiece, *The Waste Land*, we find
the definitive poetic elaboration of this same theme: the vanity of trying
to separate death from life and, at the same time, the wisdom of embracing a life that accepts, but surmounts death.[2] For Eliot, since life
and death are inseparable, only two types of characters are possible: the
typical self-centered citizen of *The Waste Land* who suffers excruciatingly
from death-in-life, and the Christian type who conquers death through
love and enjoys life-in-death.

The belief that the happiest and most desirable life is the one that
is purged of every last vestige of death, though founded on an illusion,
has won continuing acceptance throughout human history. It is reflected
in the dreams of life without aging, wealth without work, education
without effort, sex without tears, and Christianity without restraints.
Modern technological progress, which is defined in terms of exempting
us more and more from the small deaths in life, the innumerable
foreshadowings of ultimate death, gives this belief more credibility today than it ever had in the past. Yet reality, being more obdurate than
illusion, asserts its presence with ever increasing emphasis, as if it were
avenging its denial. The deliberate and concerted attempt to rid life of
all its little deaths has resulted in an unremitting assault on the very life
we seek to purify and perfect. Thus we witness with horror the counter-
productive results of our current "progress": Military might is measured
in terms of its destructive capabilities; the merger of sex with technology
leads inexorably to abortion, sterility, and impotence; synthetic drugs
render man increasingly passive and dependent; affluence increases greed
and intensifies human discontent; and the media, through its subtle but
incessant propaganda, exploits consumers with an effectiveness that has
no historic precedent.

Jacques Ellul points out in his penetrating analysis of our technical
civilization, *The Technological Society,* that its two chief problems are:
1) to perfect mechanical techniques; and 2) to invent and impose certain
human techniques so as to obviate the human sources of friction.[3] The
"technological society," according to Ellul, demands the anesthetizing
of certain human sensibilities in order to assist man in adapting to the
all important machine with which he is to co-operate with ever-increasing
efficiency. Ellul sees the fate of modern man as being encased in an ever-
broadening technological framework, a phenomenon he describes as

"technological anesthesia". In this state, man would adjust to a mechanical world, but at the price of surrendering the conflict he needs for creative consciousness.

In a similar vein, Rollo May discusses a not uncommon occurrence where an individual, in the interest of improving his sexual technique, applies an anesthetic ointment to his sex organ in order to delay orgasm. In such cases the individual chooses to feel less in order to perform better. May underscores the contradictory and self-defeating character of such a choice by remarking that "the lover who is most efficient will also be the one who is impotent."[4] Orgasm—itself an intimation of death—is delayed, but only by reducing one's experience of sexual pleasure. The ideal of mechanical efficiency in sexual intercourse, therefore, demands the sacrifice of one's own capacity to feel. Consequently, it demands impotence.

When techniques that are employed in the interest of defeating death backfire, as they often do, they make death all the more pronounced. At times, in fact, they are nothing more than death itself in thin disguise, a point sociologist George Gilder enunciates when he states that "Death often appears in the guise of eternal youth at the ever-infatuating fountains: alcohol, drugs, hallucinogenic sex."[5] The illusion that death can be separated from life denies the perennial paradox of the human predicament. Authentic human living demands accepting the inescapable conflict of life and death. But living in today's society demands acceptance of a second level of conflict: between the individual who struggles to achieve personal authenticity and the "anesthetic society" which opposes him at every turn.

Marshall McLuhan has explained at length how every invention or technology is both an extension and a "self-amputation" of our physical bodies.[6] Technological progress and anesthesia, then, go hand in hand. The effort to make life easier, in many cases, makes it even more difficult. There are pills for every pain, counselling techniques for every guilt or 'hang-up', rationalizations for every pleasant vice, and liberation ideologies for anyone who wants to feel 'invincible'. Yet along with these new technologies and techniques come new occasions for self-amputation and self-estrangement. Beyond the minor tranquilizers are the major tranquilizers, the institutionalization, the electric shock treatments. Beyond chemical contraception are the side effects, the marital breakdowns, the abortions. In using technology in an attempt to purify life of death, death wins more attention than it deserves, while man often becomes more the servant of his own technology than the beneficiary he intended himself to be. At the same time, the positive elements of life become less and less noticeable.

The solution to the dilemma of our "anesthetic society" must be understood not in terms of better technologies and techniques, but in terms of values that are eminently human, the most important of which is love. The artificial technological world that reason creates can be lived in only at the price of an adjustment and adaptation that anesthetizes our centers of feeling and caring. But we must keep these centers vital and vibrant if we are to achieve our proper destiny as human persons. Reason and technology, in trying to style a life in which all death's portents are defeated, unconsciously aim at making love obsolete. In the mechanized reactions of a totally technologized society, there would be no need for love. But at the same time there would be no sense of life.

Reason, carefully surveying life's rich potential for death, finds no end of excuses not to assume risk, marry, have children, explore the unknown, help the handicapped, oppose the consensus, or face one's own death. Reason seeks to reduce the likelihood of death by conceiving and implementing strategies against its possible occurrence. Yet neither death nor any of its prefigurements can be eradicated; they can only be denied and man's sensibility to them temporarily anesthetized.

Thomas Merton calls attention to the moral truism that the reconciliation of death with life is necessary for the preservation of the very meaning of life:

> Life comes into being without any invitation of our own. We suddenly find ourselves in it. And as soon as we recognize ourselves as alive we become aware that we tend toward inevitable death. If we do not gain some adequate understanding of our life and death, during the life-span that is ours, our life will become nothing but a querulous refusal, a series of complaints that it must end in death. Then the fear of death becomes so powerful that it results in a flat refusal of life. Life itself becomes a negation, a neurosis, a frivolity.[7]

The Christian should be well armed against the illusions of the "anesthetic society". For Christianity is a religion which views human existence primarily in terms of struggle—one that is symbolized by the archetypal conflict between our original state of sin (death) and the possibilities of grace (life). Moreover, the Christian knows that it is only by our struggle against constantly appearing false ideas that we enlarge and clarify truth, and only in our conflict with heresy that we develop and sustain the orthodoxy that is required to meet the real needs of our time.

In addition, the Christian knows that the cross, which symbolizes the intersecting conflict of life and death, has redemptive meaning. "Paganism declared that virtue was in a balance," observed Chesterton, but "Christianity declared it was in a conflict: the collision of two passions apparently opposite . . . a strong desire to live taking the form of a readiness to die."[8]

This book is a series of thirteen essays, each focussing on a specific sphere of morality where the conflict between life and death is particularly intense. Each of these essays concerns itself with the current widespread attempt on the part of our "anesthetic society" to eliminate conflict by eliminating a root element of conflict, the death element. The conflicts discussed involve: 1) Technology and Nature; 2) Commerce and Self-Denial; 3) Society and Pain; 4) The Person and Imperfection; 5) Life and Difficulty; 6) Freedom and Restriction; 7) Marriage and Sacrifice; 8) The Unborn and Finitude; 9) Sex and Incompleteness; 11) Intimacy and Self-Abandonment; 12) Fidelity and Irreversibility; 13) Morality and Guilt.

Concerning each of these moral spheres, our greatest need is not to eliminate the death element but to accept it, through love, as an inseparable part of living. Only through accepting conflict and respecting the real inseparability of its life and death elements can we begin to achieve the authentic personal wholeness that is our proper destiny.

NOTES

[1]William Blake, *Complete Poetry and Selected Prose of John Donne and Complete Poetry of William Blake* (New York: Modern Library, 1941), p. 598. "Joy & Woe are woven fine, / A clothing for the Soul divine."

[2]T.S. Eliot, *The Complete Poems and Plays 1909-1950* (New York: Harcourt, Brace & World, 1952), p. 37. "April is the cruellest month, breeding

/ Lilacs out of the dead land, mixing / Memory and desire, . . . "

[3]Jacques Ellul, *The Technological Society*, tr. John Wilkinson (New York: Knopf, 1964), p. 414.

[4]Rollo May, *Love and Will* (New York: Norton, 1969), p. 55.

[5]George Gilder, *Naked Nomads* (New York: Quadrangle, 1974), p. 142.

[6]Marshall McLuhan, *Understanding Media: The Extensions of Man* (New York: McGraw-Hill, 1964), pp. 51-56.

[7]Thomas Merton, *Love and Living* (New York: Bantam, 1979), p. 85 .

[8]G.K. Chesterton, *Orthodoxy* (Garden City: Doubleday, 1957), p. 92.

1.
Technology and the Denial of Nature

The bigger we got the more unreality we had to face.
—John Lennon

Technology is the means by which we perform a task using objects that are not part of our body. When we crack walnuts with our teeth, we are being natural. When we use a nutcracker to get the job done, we are being technological. By re-shaping the material in the world around us to assist us in accomplishing our purposes, we extend our natural powers so that we can do things which we either could not do naturally or could not do as easily. The automobile extends our ability to walk; the telescope extends our power of sight; and the computer extends certain capacities of our minds. Lewis Mumford, in his book *The City in History*,[1] speaks of the walls of the walled city as an extension—like clothing and housing—of the skin of its inhabitants.

But every technology produces a counter effect inasmuch as it tends to numb us to the very nature it extends. As we increase our reliance on the automobile for the purpose of getting from one place to another, not only do we begin to rely less on our own legs, but we become less aware that we have legs. As our industrial society conditions us toward greater dependency on things, it also increases our alienation from nature—both nature in general as well as our own specific nature as human beings.

The ancients were well aware of this problem. Plato, for example, warned that improvements in recording technologies would inevitably be accompanied by a reduction in the use of our memories as well as their gradual impairment. And this was no minor observation on his part, for Plato made it clear that a philosopher must have a good memory.

The more automated our society, the less autonomous its citizens; and the assumed goal of technological progress is to bring about a state in which machines do everything and we do nothing. It is not mere rhetoric, therefore, to ask whether Things are not already in the saddle, riding Man. We find this peculiar reversal exquisitely symbolized on the cover of a *New York* magazine whose feature essay is entitled, "Notes on the New Paralysis." The cover shows a youngster in a wheelchair while his rich mother boasts: "Of course he can walk. Thank God he doesn't have to."[2]

The extraordinary predominance of technology in the present era has created the impression that technology has gone far beyond merely *extending* nature and is now attempting to *replace* it. Some scientists, for example, have confidently asserted that it will soon be possible to produce in people a conviction or impression of happiness—through drugs or by electrical stimulation—without there being any real, natural basis for it.[3] Rather than see technology as an art that extends nature, they prefer to see it as a means of replacing nature or creating it anew.

As human beings, however, we are rooted in nature. The notion that technology could give us a new identity, one no longer rooted in nature, contradicts an ineradicable feature of our essential being. As Martin Heidegger warns, the great issue modern technology presents "is the saving of man's essential nature."

Because technology has profoundly altered the way we understand our relationship with nature, the real relationship between man, nature and art becomes problematic. Aristotle, whose thought represents the crowning achievement of the common sense realism of the ancient Greek mind, saw clearly that we are rooted in nature. But he also saw that nature does not contain us and that we are free to extend—through art—what nature has left unfinished. When he stated that "art imitates nature,"[5] he implied that art completed, perfects, and extends nature. Technology, in particular, is the art of *extending* nature by applying scientific laws to our practical purposes.

As Aristotle observed, we are neither copiers who produce nothing new, nor creators who produce what is new from nothing, but *makers* whose "making" or "work" co-operates with the creation that already exists as nature. Consequently, we cannot "make" anything unless we understand nature and obey her laws. We can work only *with* nature, not *without* her, for nature supplies both the protoplasm and the principles for everything that we produce. And because our own roots are in nature, technological art serves as a useful instrument in extending the life that nature has bequeathed us.

The idea of using art to replace nature creates the captivating illusion that we are free from the narrow limitations nature has set for us, free to enjoy new and virtually limitless experiences. Thus, the traditional view that our identity and happiness are related to our fundamental "human nature" now threatens to give way to the contemporary view that our identity and happiness can be extended to something completely removed from nature.

The prospect of a technologically induced, automatic happiness is attractive because it promises to exempt us from the need to struggle. Yet the need to struggle is rooted in our essential nature as human beings. We cannot be happy if we do not possess ourselves, and we cannot possess ourselves if we reject needs that are fundamental to our nature.

Goethe's protest that "Nature has neither core nor skin; she's both at once outside and in," reminds us that nature is everywhere. There can be no substitute for nature. She is inescapable. Technology may serve the needs of human life in countless invaluable ways, but it cannot replace human life with a synthetic or artificial version of its own.

The current problem, pervasive in scope, involves the illusion that technology, by extending nature to the point where the resulting products or images are completely dissociated from their roots in nature, actually "replaces" nature. Accordingly, technology is regarded more and more as fundamental or originative, and nature (like the "Mother Nature" of margarine commercials who is embarrassed by a product that tastes better than butter) either obsolete or rapidly receding into obsolescence. This apparent triumph of technology over nature is implied in Susan Sontag's comment that "reality has come to seem more and more like what we are shown by cameras;"[6] and Daniel Boorstin's remark that people "talk constantly not of things themselves, but of their images."[7]

Many technological extensions of our day are indeed most entrancing, especially those that offer the illusion of freedom from the "limitations of nature." Consequently people are strongly tempted to attach themselves to technologies, adapt to their mode of operating, and identify personally with them. Those who succumb to this temptation can only become increasingly insensitive to their own nature and real identity as persons. By adapting their life to technological extensions they unwittingly re-enact the tragedy of Narcissus.

According to the ancient Greek fable, Narcissus was an extremely beautiful but excessively proud youth. Nemesis, the goddess of vengeance, punished him for spurning Echo's love by causing him to fall in love with his reflection, which he saw in the silvery water of a clear fountain. He made so complete an adaptation to this naturally extended image of himself that it became his sole reality. He became numb to all else. While he gazed unceasingly at his fugitive image, which could only mirror his loving gestures, he experienced the full force of his punishment: to feel what it is to love and receive no love in return. Echo tried to lure him out of his trance by repeating fragments of his speech, but in vain. Only death succeeded in separating him from the object of his obsession. Narcissus died beside the fountain and from his remains grew the narcissus plant.

It is essential to understanding the myth to know that Narcissus did not perceive his repeated image to be himself; he interpreted it as being the reality of another. Narcissus thought his image was some beautiful water-spirit living in the fountain. The fable conveys the important point that we can be so beguiled by an extended image of ourselves—which we perceive as a lovable "other" (the other we would like to be)—that we can easily forget who we really are and thus become incapable of functioning realistically; and in the end, our preference for our image is a preference for death. Narcissus' tragedy is two-fold: that the object of his only love is incapable of receiving or returning his love; and that he is numb to all other realities. Narcissus' sole faith is in an illusion.

Here etymology is instructive. The words *Narcissus* and *narcosis* are both derived from the Greek word *nárké*, meaning "numbness." *Nárké* also designates the sedative effect of the narcissus plant. Narcissus, then, is benumbed to his real identity by the affection he has for his extended image. He becomes, in effect, an anonymity subserving an illusion. The universal implication is clear: anyone who is numb to his own identity becomes incapable of discriminating between what he is and what he is not. Marshall McLuhan, assessing the Narcissus myth, remarks that "it is, perhaps, indicative of the bias of our intensely technological and, therefore, narcotic culture that we have long interpreted the Narcissus story to mean that he fell in love with himself, that he imagined the reflection to be Narcissus!"[8]

The Narcissus myth has an important application to our technological society where it is commonplace for people to have strong attachments for their technologically extended images. And the fact that narcissism is a predominant feature of our society is well documented in Christopher Lasch's book, *The Culture of Narcissism*, where he remarks that, "Narcissism appears realistically to represent the best way of coping with the tensions and anxieties of modern life, and the prevailing social conditions therefore tend to bring out narcissistic traits that are present, in varying degrees, in everyone."[9]

Take television, for example, where there seems to be a symbolic re-enactment of the vengeance of Nemesis: The narcissistic televiewer sees the objects of his affections "mirrored" on a silvery screen without there being any possibility that they could ever be concerned about him! Through such emotional attachment to technologically extended images of himself, he repeats the experience of Narcissus, loving what cannot love in return, while mistaking it for a substantial reality.

Consider also the much discussed relationships that some movie stars, television celebrities, and sports heroes have for their media-extended images. It is well known that these images commonly bear little or no resemblance to the actual people behind the images. The typical question that movie magazines ask—"What is Paul Newman *really* like?"— more than suggests this mysterious gulf that separates the private person from the public "persona." But the life-adjustment problems of unemployed actors, over-exposed television personalities, and retired athletes who have become used to the intoxicating effect of their public images are akin to the withdrawal pains (or "cold turkey") that drug-dependent individuals suffer when their drugs are withdrawn. Being a "big name" star can be a dangerous "high," numbing an individual to his or her identity.

It belongs to the very nature of the media to require extreme sacrifices of people on the personal level for the sake of their images. Fashion models mortify themselves severely so that they can photograph better. Stunt men are sometimes obliged to brush with death in order to provide a bit of sensationalism for movie viewers. Actresses are commonly advised to abort when they have untimely pregnancies, and to have plastic surgery when time shows too plainly on their faces. Marilyn Monroe asks her biographer to "love me for my yellow hair alone."[10] The media, which routinely ridicules moral asceticism, is curiously solemn and rigorous in its demands for image asceticism. In many cases the media's ascetic requirements actually run counter to an individual's well-being. The actor who played Brother Dominic for Xerox commercials, for example, was required by contract to be very much overweight so that he could play the role of a portly monk more convincingly. For the film, *Raging Bull*, Robert DeNiro put on fifty pounds so that he could play the role of Jake LaMotta, an overweight retired boxer, more realistically.

While the split between person and persona is plainly evident in the lives of mass media celebrities, the same phenomenon is widespread among ordinary people, although it receives proportionally less notoriety; the quiet desperation of the undistinguished is simply not as newsworthy as the alcoholism of a former astronaut. But we do read in the daily press of the tragic results of countless individuals who try to live exclusively in technologically extended images of themselves: A St. Paul youth of fifteen years commits suicide because of the cancellation of his favorite TV show, *Battlestar Galactica*. A 16-year-old Canadian kills himself because his parents ask him to wait a year or two before he gets his driver's license. A 17-year-old Illinois high school student dies while inhaling butane lighter fluid in an attempt to ignite it and breathe fire in imitation of his idols of the rock group, "Kiss". We read of adults who do away with themselves because of a sudden loss of wealth or because circumstances require them to part with some important material possession such as a business or a house.

In each of these cases death resulted because people loved themselves too little and their images—the others they wanted to be like—too much. Love transforms the lover into the object he loves: love for an image that has no personal reality is necessarily depersonalizing; love for an image that has no substantial reality can be fatal. If an individual allows himself to form, through his love, a strong identification with a TV image and that image is cancelled (the television equivalent of death), then it becomes understandable why that individual might experience withdrawal symptoms and possibly even think of suicide. Unrequited love for an image lacks the stabilizing realism of reciprocal love, which is anchored in the personal realities of the lovers, and represents nothing more than a hopeless infatuation with a technological illusion.

We gain a feel of the pandemic popularity of ordinary individuals extending themselves into current technologies by consulting contemporary folk humor. Folk humor is a natural way (sometimes the only way) of dealing with grievances. It frequently expresses the inherent absurdity of a situation more concisely and forcefully than any other means available. The grievance man has concerning the strange sense of self-alienation technology has produced in him is evident from the following citations: A teenager says to her examining doctor, "Oh, it's my hearing—that's a relief, I thought my amplifier was going!" A woman answers a friend who just complimented her young child by saying, "That's nothing, wait 'til you see his photograph!" An athlete remarks, "I won't know if I'm injured until I study the game films." A doctor tells his patient, "I'm sorry, Mr. Jones, there's nothing I can do for you; but I can touch up your X-rays."

Commercial advertising, which is technology's sales bureau, is not satisfied with merely exhibiting its wares; it must get people to identify with its products. In most cases the identification is subtle and indirect, but in other cases it is undisguised. Thus, a whole class of human beings who consume a particular soft drink belong to the "Pepsi Generation". The Tareyton smoker's black eye is not only proof of his loyalty to that brand but is an actual part of his physical identity. A fully modern woman states in an ad for condoms: "My man is a Shield's Man." We hear of "Marlboro Men," "Clairol Women," and "Maytag Families". The examples are numerous and all such ads fully exploit technology as a means of selling people new identities for old.

Every form of narcissism has its built-in subtleties which make it difficult to diagnose. The subtlety of today's narcissism that is connected with technology is the fact that it involves a large group of people at the same time. In the original myth, narcissism is a solitary phenomenon; in a technocracy, it affects virtually everyone at once. Daniel Boorstin, in his book *The Republic of Technology*, makes the point that "Every year our nation becomes less peculiar."[11] He argues that because of technology, the experience of Americans becomes increasingly the same. On a particular Sunday afternoon, for example, nearly 100 million Americans will share the common experience of watching two football teams compete for glory in the annual Super Bowl classic. The winner of this contest will aptly symbolize to this same group of people what is eminently desirable in a technological society: supremacy, power, fame, and abundant financial reward. These values, extended by technology on a mass level, do not conform to man's more elementary natural needs (Freud correctly recognized that wealth cannot satisfy man because it is not based on an infantile wish). Moreover, as group ideals they are contradictory since not everyone can be number one, and more powerful, famous, and wealthy than most others.

One of the telling traits of the solitary narcissist is precisely his isolation from others. Usually only the narcissist himself would be in a position to defend his peculiar outlook. But group narcissism is protected by the fact that it is defended by everyone in that group; it is not regarded as peculiar as long as its values are shared by many. Although it is insulated from reality, it is not isolated from other people. Its vocabulary of "we" rather than "I", "our nation" rather than "myself" gives it an aura of altruism; the fact that it represents a consensus offers the semblance of truth and creates the impression of rational comportment.

Erich Fromm speaks of a form of "low-grade chronic schizophrenia"[12] that can be a pathological, though difficult to detect, characteristic of a large group of people. As long as millions of people share the same sickness, according to Fromm, they feel a certain strength in numbers which reassures them of being perfectly healthy. Group narcissism, therefore, is a pathology that is not only difficult for the afflicted multitude to detect, but as it progresses, its detection becomes increasingly unlikely.

Gabriel Marcel makes the point in his book *Man Against Mass Society*[13] that "a man cannot be free or remain free, except in the degree to which he remains linked with that which transcends him." The bane of all narcissistic groups is their loss of contact with that which is outside of them. The neurotic individual, for Freud, suffered because he failed to adapt successfully to his society. The Freudian individual has now graduated to the point where he happily adapts to the societal system, but still suffers because, in forming a closed relationship with that system, he has cut himself off from that which exists outside of the system. Jacques Ellul argues that in the technological society, the purpose of psychological methods is "to neutralize or eliminate aberrant individuals and tendencies to fractionalization;" and that "man is to be smoothed out, like a pair of pants under a steam iron."[14] Today's societal discontent is simply a manifestation of the next developed stage of yesterday's individual discontent. Man's personal destiny, however, is always to remain open to the transcendent. No closed system society, no matter how sophisticated and etherealized its technology, can satisfy his personal needs and desires.

The essential paradox concerning the inter-relationships between man, nature, and art is that as long as art serves man by working in harmony with nature, his life continues to improve and continues to remain open to the infinite; but when art tries to emancipate itself from nature, it can provide man only some fixed and narrow image which inevitably immobilizes him. Perhaps the best explanation of this paradox is what it was the Greek genius to intuit, namely, that nature, because of its dynamic character, intimates the infinite, whereas everything that man grasps as an image he perceives as circumscribed and therefore finite.

The passage from solitary to group narcissism bears an analogical relationship with the passage from psychoanalysis to social psychology and the study of the masses. The expression "sick society" has come into vogue, replacing, to a certain extent, the idea of the individual alone being sick. The French psychologist Le Bon was the first student of mass psychology. He drew the conclusion that the mass, acting as a group, was capable of acting in a more bestial manner than all the single individuals who compose the group. Freud, in studying Le Bon's ideas, stated that the mass possesses only an *id* but not an *ego*.[15] For the contemporary inhabitant of mass society who rigorously conforms to its impersonal values, *id* becomes his I.D.. Lewis Mumford, speaking in this vein, has discussed the emergence of "megatechnic primitivism"[16]—the negative correlative of megatechnic society—that made its most pronounced appearance as Woodstock Nation. "Megatechnic primitivism"[16]—adheres to the same materialistic values as does the mass society against which it supposedly revolts, but combines its addiction to cars, drugs, stereos, and the mass taste that is exemplified by fashionable discs and films, with a return to the Great Outdoors, herding in large groups, living in unhygienic conditions, and public sex. This counter-culture is connected by invisible electrodes to the same pecuniary and libidinal centers from which spring the dreams that characterize the establishment's group narcissism. It does not revolt against the establishment, but merely provides an immature imitation of it.

Technology unifies the members of mass society, standardizes their life, and gives them common goods and similar experiences. But as it accomplishes all these tasks, it tends to dissolve individual relationships with the transcendent. Categories of the sacred and the sublime cease to have strong and immediate meaning for people. Religion declines or makes accommodation with technology's materialistic implications. The poet is replaced by the computer, and the clergyman by a psychotechnician. As the technological society becomes more and more efficient and self-sufficient, it moves toward an automated society whose proper name, as Mumford remarks, "is self-inflicted impotence."[17] Terminology that was once restricted to psychological descriptions of individual pathologies is now readily applied to society in general. Mumford goes on to state that the technologically automated society is "a neat mechanical model of a compulsion neurosis, and perhaps even springs from the same ultimate source—anxiety and insecurity."[18]

The dream of the individual that his life could run automatically like an efficient machine, has begun to assume the proportions of a corporate nightmare in which automation unleashes its suffocating powers of standardization, over-regimentation, and depersonalization. Arthur Miller's trenchant remark that we live in an "air conditioned nightmare," implies the unhappy co-existence of technological progress and spiritual regress. Like real nightmares, it takes place within a profound collective sleep, therefore offering many little chance of discovering either its cause or its cure.

The machine serves us only as long as it is subordinated to our needs. When we come to identify ouselves or our life in terms of our mechanical extensions, the machine no longer serves us, but we it. Because the machine is not alive, it is inferior to us in a most fundamental and important way; ultimately it oppresses us rather than rejuvenates us. The machine is also fixed and determined. In this regard, it is unable to offer us a sense of the transcendent that is vitally needed to nourish our spiritual centers. Fromm warns that an excessive interest in the mechanical, in something that is not alive, leads to an attraction to death or, in its less drastic forms, to an indifference toward life instead of "reverence for life."[19] His point is well taken: machines can only run down; they cannot operate counter to the law of entropy and grow and evolve as living things can and do. Hence, the wearying effect that comes with working too long with machines. Compare, for example, the expressions on the faces of workers in an automotive plant with those of nurses in a maternity ward.

Technology promises to make our life easier, and in innumerable evident ways it fulfills these promises. In one beneficial way, computers relieve us from trivial and laborious work so that we can direct our minds toward more challenging enterprises. But a critical point is reached when we permit technology to substitute for our own fundamental, meditative thinking about our personal identity, for example, or our moral obligations to others, or our place in the world. Aristotle pointed out that thinking means suffering, since it cannot take place without reason's suffering. It is equally true that there can be no moral consciousness in the absence of suffering. Dostoevsky confessed that the one thing he feared above all else was that he would not be worthy of his suffering. T.S. Eliot, as a poet, prided himself on what he referred to as "that peculiar honesty which, in a world too frightened to be honest, is peculiarly terrifying." We distinguish ourselves from the mass and the machine by our willingness to accept the pain and the struggle that are an inseparable part of our personal growth.

Technology can have an anesthetic effect on man, dulling his moral consciousness and his capacity to enter into fundamental, meditative thinking. One of the more familiar ways technology produces this effect is through motion, especially rapid motion. "Speed", from drag races to drugs, offers man the illusion of being absolved from the need to think, and from all the conflicts and suffering that thinking entails. Friedrich Juenger notes in *The Failure of Technology* that motion has a narcotic attraction for technological man, "particularly where the going is fast, where speed is record breaking."[20] Tommaso Marinetti served advance notice to the present generation's intoxication with speed in his *Initial Manifesto of Futurism* where he wrote: "We declare that the world's

splendour has been enriched by a new beauty, the beauty of speed....
Already we live in the absolute, since we have already created speed,
eternal and ever-present.''[21]

Speed is inversely related not only to our awareness of living, but
to the frequency and quality of our interpersonal experiences. In walking to work we gather along the way a host of interpersonal experiences.
If we use a bicycle, these experiences are fewer; and if we use the
automobile, they are fewer still. At an ideal of instant speed, the number
of such experiences would be reduced to zero. Paradoxically, at high
speeds, our life would become impoverished for lack of human exchanges, our world would become static. One pragmatist philosopher,
in attempting to justify this form of idealizing speed, stated that the ''going
becomes the goal.'' Nonetheless, such a dictum accords technology more
centrality than it deserves and accords living less centrality than common sense demands. And in the reassertion of common sense we may
find almost effective antidote to the inhuman tendencies of our anesthetic
society.

Speed as an end in itself, then, tends to narcotize man to life's content and inclines him toward the fate of Narcissus. Speed is only one
example, though a salient and important one, of how technology ceases
to be man's ally when it becomes an end in itself. Through history, speed,
power, and control have been the three chief marks of every absolute
monarchy. We see this triumvirate today enshrined as the chief marks
of absolute technocracy . The automobile—the most typical triumph of
mass production in the technological society—virtually embodies speed
and power (and control to a lesser degree). But since 1900, the automobile
has killed more people than have been killed in all the wars ever fought
by the United States.[22] The affinity between technology and death is evident there. At the same time, however technology has an equivalent affinity for life. The differentiating factor is whether technology serves
the person, assisting in his care, development, and freedom, or the person chooses to serve technology, thereby narcotizing himself to his own
superior personal value while planting himself in the fatal footsteps of
Narcissus.

In Zen Buddhism there is a simple proverb which reads: ''to point
at the moon a finger is needed, but woe to those who take the finger
for the moon.'' The image here may seem unduly quaint, but it em-

phasizes the philosophical principle all the more beautifully: it is always absurd, no matter what the technique, to use an instrument to occlude man's vision. Technology serves man as an instrument, just as the finger is a suitable instrument for pointing at the moon. As long as technology is subordinate to man, the right means works for the right end and man is the beneficiary. In this regard, Aristotle's imitative notion of art is upheld. But in fixating attention on technology, or the finger, one permits the means to usurp the end, the finger to eclipse the moon, technology to rule the man. "Woe to those" who are mesmerized by means and are crushed under its oppressive weight. Man's destiny is always to look beyond. When the astronauts achieved the moon, their attention ws soon re-directed to the clarity of the untwinkling stars which they saw through vacuous space. If the moon landing proved anything to the astronauts, it proved that every new technology is outshined by the more glorious natural wonders it reveals. The universe is too rich and versatile to allow technology to be an end. Narcissus, on the other hand, chose the static journey to nowhere, fully narcotized to the transcendent inner self to which infinity beckoned from beyond. Art imitates nature, but nature intimates the infinite.

NOTES

[1]Lewis Mumford, *The City in History* New York: Harcourt, 1961).

[2]*New York*, 28 October 1970.

[3]See Jacques Ellul, *The Technological Society*, (New York: Random House, 1964), pp. 428-436. See also Erich Fromm, *The Revolution of Hope* (New York Harper & Row, 1968), p. 44 "But the idea that it [the computer] replaces man and life is the manifestation of the pathology of today."

[4]Martin Heidegger, *Discourse on Thinking* (New York: Harper & Row, 1966), p. 56.

[5]*Exposition of the Posterior Analytics, Prologue.*

[6]Susan Sontag, "Photography Unlimited," *New York Review*, 23 June 1977, pp. 26, 28, 31.

[7]Daniel Boorstin, *The Image: A Guide to Pseudo-Events in America* (New York: Atheneum, 1972), p. 204.

[8]Marshall McLuhan, *Understanding Media: The Extensions of Man* (New York: New American Library, 1964), pp. 51-5. McLuhan argues that as man adapts to his extension of himself he suffers a corresponding "auto-amputation" and concludes that "Self-amputation forbids self-recognition."

[9]Christopher Lasch, *The Culture of Narcissism* (New York: W.W. Norton Co., 1979), p. 101.

[10]Norman Rosten, *Marilyn, An Untold Story* (New York: New American Library, 1973).

[11]Daniel Boorstin, *The Republic of Technology* (New York: Harper & Row, 1978, p. xiii.

[12]Erich Fromm, p. 41.

[13]Gabriel Marcel, *Man Against Mass Society* (Chicago: Henry Regnery, 1962), p. 23.

[14]Ellul, pp. 410-11

[15]See Karl Stern, *Love and Success* (New York: Farrar, Straus, & Giroux, 1975). p. 110.

[16]Lewis Mumford, *The Myth of the Machine: the Pentagon of Power* (New York: Harcourt, Brace, & Jovanovich, 1964), p. 373. " . . . despite their gestures of revolt against the established goods of civilization, the young are in fact addicted to its most decadent mass products [radio and television happenings, etc.]. This is purely megatechnic primitivism."

[17]*Ibid.,* p. 184.

[18]*Ibid.,* p. 185.

[19]Fromm, p. 42.

[20]Friedrich Juenger, *The Failure of Technology* (Chicago: Regenery, 1956), p. 172.

[21]In Erich Fromm, *The Heart of Man* (New York: Harper & Row, 1968), pp. 59-60. "A racing motor-car, its frame adorned with great pipes, like snakes with explosive breath . . . a roaring motor-car, which looks as though running on a shrapnel is more beautiful than the *Victory of Samothrace.*"

[22]See Mumford, *The Myth*, p. 350. See also José Ortega y Gasset, *The Revolt of the Masses* (New York: Norton, 1957), p. 81: "Of course, he [mass man] is interested in anesthetics, motor-cars, and a few other things. But this fact merely confirms his fundamental lack of interest in civilisation."

2.
Commerce and the Avoidance of Self-Denial

Money as Metaphor Translates Everything as A-greed.
—Marshall McLuhan

In 1919 a cache of early Hawaiian postage stamps, identified as the "Missionaries", was discovered in Los Angeles. The stamps were soon purchased by a dealer for $65,000. Upon studying them, the new owner came to the conclusion that they were counterfeits and immediately took action to recover what he paid for them. During the ensuing trial, which lasted fourteen days, several distinguished philatelic experts assisted in the determination of whether the "Missionaries" were priceless or worthless.

The decision of the judge was that the stamps were forgeries; thereafter he consistently referred to them as "the 43 pieces of paper". After the trial, however, further testimony was offered and new evidence advanced which, according to other experts, "proved" the "Missionaries" to be genuine.[1] Recently, one of these stamps was placed on auction and advertised "as is" with an estimated value in the range of $3,000 to $5,000. After more than half a century the 'value' of these stamps is still a matter of pure speculation.

There is something annoyingly odd about no one knowing whether an item of great popular interest is a treasure or a trifle; and, moreover, even after expert testimony has been given. But such is the commercial world of fabricated and inflated values, a world which is, nonetheless, the socio-economic world we inhabit.

"Truth is the cash value of an idea,"[2] as William James once said. He thought he was being pragmatic, shifting the basis of truth from *being* to currency. But "cash value" is tied to the will of those who control the economy. In this regard, fixing prices is something like fixing a boxing match; in either case the profit motive tends to eclipse fair play. In addition, "cash value" is also tied to such daily uncertainties as the "bullish" or "bearish" mood of the market, and such persistent perplexities as the "world situation" or "public confidence". Leon Bloy was right when he remarked that the world of finance is a peculiar kind of mystery play.[3] Severed from enduring intrinsic values, market-values are incomprehensible as well as upredictable.

In a more realistic perspective, on the other hand, a natural proportion exists between value and response to that value. We love something because it is good. We marvel at something because it is wondrous. To put it even more simply, we love what is lovable, we admire what is admirable. Without hinting at any abstruse metaphysical distinction, let us just say that whenever we love someone or admire something, we give credit not to our own powers of perception but to what we love or admire for an excellence that belongs primarily to it. The lover does not create lovableness in another, he discovers it, and to the degree his love is pure, it is free from ulterior motives.

The commercial world, however, pivots not on metaphysical principles such as goodness and love but on economic factors of supply and demand. The goodness of something—a person, let us say—is already there, intrinsic to its subject and therefore making it naturally lovable in its own right. In our socio-economic world, whenever there is an oversupply, a demand is not a natural response to that supply (the way wonder is a natural response to a plethora of stars in the sky), but one that must be created.

The task of creating a demand for something that would otherwise go ignored belongs, in the main, to commercial advertising. The task of providing the supply in the first place belongs to technology. The marriage of technology and commercial advertising, therefore, is basic for an understanding of our present economic structure. Technology creates the product; advertising creates the market. In tandem they create something called "progress". Yet it is a form of progress that can take place without any reference to intrinsic values.

Values that were once to be found in nature (created by God) are no longer compelling against those proposed by the new amalgamation whose values, tenuous and tentative though they may be, are created by advertising. As Daniel Boorstin has remarked, "Technology is a way of multiplying the unnecessary. And advertising is a way of persuading us that we didn't know what we needed."[4] For *Homo economicus* intrinsic good is transvaluated into commercial value and nature yields to progress.

Fred Allen had an insight into the creative demands of today's advertiser when he spoke of the "mole-hill man" whose task was to make his mole-hill into a mountain by the end of his work day. The advertiser's function, creating out of nothing, gives him a certain quasi-religious aura so that when he announces, for example, that the "wet head is dead", his proclamation is uncritically accepted by the obedient masses.

In a world of floating commercial values, a right-to-life claim seems absolutistic; in a world of progress, it seems strangely out of date. According to the pre-suppositions of commercialism, every value must be subject to re-evalutaion and no value should impede the wheels of progress. (Why progress should be regarded as an absolute value, of course, is not questioned; in a system of progressive commercialism its sacrosanct character is simply taken for granted.)

Yesterday's unborn had higher market-value because a woman's reproductive period was relatively short and the infant mortality rate relatively high. With today's increased life-span and improved post-natal care (together with the presumed over-population condition), the market-value for a typical human fetus is relatively low. Thus Margaret Mead can write in *Redbook*:

> The Right to Life people, it seems to me, are tied to a past when, because women died so young their reproductive period was very short (only about 15 years in the late Middle Ages) and because so many children could not survive, there was always the danger that there might not be enough people to carry on the world's work.[5]

Of course, Dr. Mead is judging past attitudes uniformly (and sterotypically) in terms of today's progressive commercialism and is apparently unconcerned about why other people operating within different value systems (e.g. one in which the intrinsic good of the human unborn is revered) proscribed abortion. But it is rare that a person analyzes the pre-suppositions of his own philosophy. In this regard, however, I believe that Right to Life people are one up on the voluble Dr. Mead. They know that the basis of the right to life is not anything as elusive and unidentifiable as any of the sundry and nebulous factors that affect the daily Dow-Jones average. The basis for the claim that a given human life has a right to life is in that very life itself. One has a right to be because he *is* and because his existing being is a good. The right to be is consequent upon the good of being. This is not a redundancy but a comprehensive recognition of all that belongs essentially to a human-being-in-the-world. Being, value, and right-to-be all belong to the same existing human. As *being* he stands outside of nothingness and has a specific meaning; as *value* he is a natural object of love and care; as having a *right-to-be* his being and value demand protection and honor.

To Oscar Wilde's assertion that sunsets were not valued because we could not pay for them, Chesterton retorted: "We can pay for them by not being Oscar Wilde."[6] The point is this: one honors the being of man not by attaching a price to it or urging it to be something other than it is, but by encouraging it to be all that it is—to live and at the same time to be true to all the personal and moral implications that are intrinsic to its being.

The right to life, from a human point of view, is an uncreated value. It warrants our reverence not our day-to-day reappraisal. Perhaps this point offends those who have tender egos, those who prefer a world of commercial values in which they have a share in determining and controlling all values. The egoist is not interested in what he neither creates nor controls. This may help to explain why used postage stamps, empty bottles, and tin cans can be *wanted* and unborn humans *unwanted*. Junk dealers can be more appreciative of other people's junk than some mothers are of their own flesh.

Martin Heidegger begins his epoch making work, *Being and Time*, with the complaint that not only has the modern world forgotten the *being* of things but it no longer even cares.[7] Popular intelligence views the notion of *being*, the most concrete of all notions, as a meaningless abstraction. At the same time it places its trust in a "hard reality"—

money. The Russian existentialist Nicolas Berdyaev writes: "The bourgeois' most fantastic creation, the most unreal, the most uncanny and horrible in its unreality—is the kingdom of money."[8] Malcolm Muggeridge adds that money is "materialism's least convincing manifestation."[9]

In this phantasmogorical kingdom of banks, stock-exchanges, checks, credit cards, and liquidity preference, real substance and together with it, intrinsic values, disappear. Money is a medium of exchange. It has no value in itself. Hence money is metaphor, an invitation to dream about any of the needless things money can buy. It can hold a whole society together, spellbound to a dream. Money is a more intoxicating myth than paradise because of the relative immediacy with which its redemption takes place. Moreover, one does not have to die in order to reap its benefits.

The popular attitude toward property hinges on its attitude toward money. The typical citizen of modern society is defined not by what he is but by what he has. Supposedly we are all born nameless; we must *make* a name for ourselves. Hence the central importance of what Thorstein Veblen has termed "conspicuous consumption" and "pecuniary emulation".[10] Property is anything a person can *have* which adds to his personal comfort and social status. Money is the key to property. This being so in the kingdom of gracious living, how is a penniless, property-less unborn child to be defined? Since he is defined not by what he is but by what he has, he must be nothing in his own right; and, because he does exist, he must be the property of someone else and therefore subject to the same value fluctuations as any other property item. One unborn child, being judged "unwanted", might be retired; another who is wanted by the right people might fetch as a neonate $50,000 on the black baby market (although babies, unborn or newly born, are not as readily transferrable as stocks, bonds, capital, or real estate).

Justice, on the other hand, in its most elementary sense, accomplishes two things: on the positive side it honors and defends a person's right-to-be; on the negative side it protects a person from being utilized as property. A society that is devoted to property more than people is not a just society. At the recent CAPEX show in Toronto, $50,000 worth of security protected 50,000,000 of display stamps. In the United States, if one is convicted of stealing a car, he has a 75 percent chance of going to jail for an average sentence of three years. Would that the human fetus received such protection, or that God enforced as much respect for his creations as does General Motors for its. Planned Parenthood of Virginia warns expectant mothers: "Your first baby will cost as much as: 5 sports cars . . . can you afford that now? In Monaco, where a one bedroom apartment lists for $400,000 only the presence of police rivals its evident display of wealth. Says one rich resident: "It's a police state, sure, but they're our police." The apparent goal of Prince Rainier's armed force, as John Vinocur of the New York *Times* expresses it, "is letting women walk home from Cartier or Van Cleef with their new jewels ablaze—making Monaco safe for ostentation and torpor."

Perhaps nothing could better exemplify the excesses of modern materialism than a governmental plan instituted to protect the interests of American business overseas by sterilizing, over a period of nine years, about 100,000,000 women in developing countries. The plan, known as "advanced fertility management," was revealed by Dr. R.T. Ravenholt, Director of the U.S. Office of Population. "If the population explosion proceeds unchecked, said Dr. Ravenholt, it will cause such terrible economic conditions abroad that revolutions will ensue. And revolutions, he suggested, are scarcely ever beneficial to the interests of the United States."

A society that kills its own may be uncivilized, but if it safeguards its property it may still maintain its status as a "developed nation". Significantly, countries are not labelled "civilized" or "uncivilized" anymore. That distinction is based on "abstract" philosophical values that involve goodness, justice, and personal rights. Today's countries are "developed", "developing", or "under-developed" (something like the ontogeny of an athlete). The great geneticist Jerome Lejeune argues that the only true test of civilization is what a society is willing to do for its citizens who are neither wealthy nor healthy. A society devoted to commercial values regards the poor and the sick as economic liabilities. Yet, by turning away from concrete values of justice and personality that are rooted in being, a commercial society looks away from reality and, in so doing, it finally becomes preoccupied with mere images. The media, the inevitable child of the marriage of technology and advertising, is essentially a world of images. But its images, while tantalizing, are bodiless, de-individuated. They constitute a world not of substance but of *sensibilia*. They belong not to any one person but to the paying, if undiscriminating, masses.

Television multiplies images so that everyone can *have* his own set of celebrities. Humphrey Bogart is not dead, he lives on through the countless film festivals that are assembled in his honor. Death is defeated through the transformation of personal substance into public property. The conversion of intrinsic value to commmercial value is hailed as benefitting a broader range of people. Yet from Humphrey Bogart's point of view (the view the media finds irrelevant) he is surely dead. And from the spectators' point of view, they are personally deprived. One can well imagine the world coming to an end, practical imperatives having been abandoned, while the dissociated masses are being gaily entertained. Kierkegaard warned:

> It happened that a fire broke out backstage in a theatre. The clown came out to inform the public. They thought it was a jest and applauded. He repeated this warning; they shouted even louder. So I think the world will come to an end amid general applause from all the wits, who believe that it is a joke.[12]

What is objectionable about the poor and the sick is that they embody everything which the media and its progressively commercialized environment oppose. If someone is not beautiful or talented enough to be on television, he should at least be wealthy enough to own one. The unhealthy are unpleasant to look at and the unwealthy are economic burdens. They are failures on every level that society takes seriously. Small wonder that they and their right-to-life advocates are denounced in the same breath. Whereas right-to-life values are substantial, those of the media are imaginary; whereas right-to-life values are grounded in intrinsic worth, those of our modern world are attached to floating commercial values.

When pro-abortionists decry the fire-bombings of abortion clinics while approving the human carnage that routinely takes place when those clinics are functioning, they are one with the thinking that now finds its most concrete expression in the highly sophisticated Neutron Bomb, which destroys people without jeopardizing property. It is no wonder that Kierkegaard saw fastidiousness as the besetting sin of the modern world, the preference for the unblemished form over the blemished man. Alternatively, Max Weber analyzed capitalism as a mad drive to acquire the self-sufficient. It may very well be true that modern society is in love with the perfect and the self-sufficient. But inasmuch as it pursues these ideals apart from substance and intrinsic value, that is, apart from finite, blemished human beings, it pursues them apart from justice and love. It is not, after all, the unwanted babies, or the poor, or the sick that impede progress. Rather, as T.S. Eliot expresses it so magnificently:

> Garlic and sapphires in the mud
> Clot the bedded axle-tree.[13]

In this light, a society in pursuit of painless self-sufficiency—a fastidious society—is seen as aesthetic rather than loving. Its commercial values fail to embrace the fundamental life-death tension of human existence. In a word, its conception of Christ is completed at Cana rather that at Calvary.

NOTES

[1]Henry A. Meyer, Frederic R. Harris, et al., *Hawaii: Its Stamps and Postal History* (Philatelic Foundation, 1948).

[2]William James, "How We Know," *The Philosophy of William James* (New York: Random House, n.d.), p. 190. See also Will Durant, *The Story of Philosophy* (New York: Simon & Schuster, 1959), p. 518: "Certainly, as everyone has pointed out, the manner, if not the substance, of James's thinking was specifically and uniquely American. The American lust for movement and acquisition fills the sails of his style and thought, and gives them a buoyant and almost aerial motility. Huneker calls it "a philosophy for philistines," and indeed there is something that smacks of salesmanship in it: James talks of God as of an article to be sold to a materialistically-minded consumer by every device of optimistic advertising; and he counsels us to believe as if he were recommending long-term investments, with high dividends, in which there was nothing to lose, and all the (other) world to win."

[3]Leon Bloy, *Le salut par les Juifs.*

[4]Daniel Boorstin, "Tomorrow: the Republic of Technology," *Time*, January 17, 1977, p. 23.

[5]Margaret Mead, "The Many Rights to Life," *Redbook*, July, 1978 p. 174.

[6]G.K. Chesterton, *Orthodoxy* (Garden City: Doubleday, 1959), p. 58.

[7]Martin Heidegger, *Being and Time*, tr. John Macquarrie and Edward Robin-

son (New York: Harper & Row, 1962), p.1

[8]Nicolas Berdyaev, *Slavery and Freedom* (New York: Scribner, 1944), p. 185. See also Berdyaev, *The Destiny of Man* (New York: Harper & Row, 1960), pp. 182-3.

[9]Malcolm Muggeridge, "Why We Face a Decade of Lost Utopias," London *Sunday Telegraph*, December 30, 1979. Reprinted in *The Human Life Review*, Vol. VI, No. 1, Winter 1980, p. 123.

[10]Thorstein Veblen, *The Theory of the Leisure Class* (New York: The New American Library, 1953), Chapters 4 and 5.

[11]Jeremy Campbell, the London *Evening Standard*, "Washington Newsletter," Dec. 5, 1977. Reprinted in part in *Christian Order*, Vol. 19, March 1978, pp. 130-132.

[12]See Richard M. Weaver, *Ideas Have Consequences* (Chicago: University of Chicago Press, 1971), p. 185.

[13]T.S. Eliot, *Four Quartets,* "burnt Norton," section II. In the Address of His Holiness Pope John Paul II to the XXIV General Assembly of the United Nations Organization, 2 Oct., 1979, n. 15, the Holy Father said: "A critical analysis of our modern civilization shows that in the last hundred years it has contributed as never before to the development of material goods, but that it has also given rise, both in theory and still more in practice, to a series of attitudes in which sensitivity to the spiritual dimension of human existence is diminished to a greater or less extent, as a result of certain premises which reduce the meaning of human life chiefly to the many different material and economic factors—I mean to the demands of production, the market, consumption, the accumulation of riches or of the growing bureaucracy with which an attempt is made to regulate these very processes.

3.
Society and the Elimination of Pain

Anybody can be virtuous now. You can carry at least half your morality about in a bottle. Christianity without tears—that's what soma *is.*
—Aldous Huxley, *Brave New World*

Tranquility, like peace, happiness, freedom, and all other qualities of the soul that man ardently seeks to attain, is ambiguous. It is calmness and nothing more, what Alfred North Whitehead calls "the negative conception of anesthesia."[1] Or it is calmness combined with "a positive feeling which crowns the 'life and motion' of the soul."[2] In this sense Wordsworth saw the origin of poetry as "emotion recollected in tranquility,"[3] Edna St. Vincent Millay described human beauty as "the tranquil blossom on the tortured stem,"[4] and St. Augustine viewed tranquility as the peace-conferring characteristic of man's life in moral order.[5] Tranquility, then, describes both the enervated and the active, the quiescent and the creative. It is both incompatible and compatible with motion and emotion. Consequently, the search for tranquility leads either to anesthesia, or to a life that abounds in movement and meaning.

The popular predilection is to seek the kind of tranquility that is readily induced—anesthesia—and drug companies, being more than opportunistic, have mass produced tranquility in a pill. The business relationship that has eventuated over the past few decades between the pill companies and the public has been stupendously successful.

In the past generation tranquilizers, antidepressants and sedatives, most of which were unknown before the early fifties, have become the most powerful and extensive technology of mood and behavior control ever employed in a democratic nation. By 1971 the pharmaceutical industry was spending, according to the Social Security Administration, about $1 billion a year to promote these drugs, roughly $5,000 per practicing physician (at the same time American medical schools were spending a total of $977 million for all their educational activities). By 1975 American physicians were writing 240 million annual pharmacy prescriptions for psychotropic drugs for people who were not hospitalized, enough to sustain a $1.5 billion industry and to keep every American fully medicated for a month.[6] In this same year tranquilizers were prescribed more than 100 million times to an estimated 30 million people: 61 million prescriptions were written for Valium alone, the nation's most popular tranquilizer with annual sales at about $500 million; 17 million for Librium; and 25 million for other minor tranquilizers. In all, enough to provide some 15 million pills a day, and at a rate that is increasing by 5 or 6 million prescriptions a year.[7]

In Canada, the situation is more temperate—1,151,600 prescriptions for Valium in 1978, representing a commercial value of $5,539,000—but still intemperate enough to prompt the Canadian Medical Association's late secretary-general J.D. Wallace to say: "It's a tranquilizer on demand syndrome. There's a feeling by the patient that he has a right to a prescription. And doctors with not the time to talk people out of the idea, give in. It's the fad of the century,"[8]

Dependence on prescribed tranquilizers has risen by 290 per cent since 1962.[9] For fifteen years, drug industry profits (as a percentage of sales and company net worth) have out-performed those of all other manufactured industries listed in the Stock Exchange. In all but two of the years between 1956 and 1971 the pharmaceutical industry was the most profitable industry in the United States.[10] Valium and Librium have earned millions of dollars for its inventors, Swiss-based Hoffman-La Roche, and have made it the largest drug company in the world, a single share currently selling for more than $35,000. In the United States drugs that affect the central nervous system represent the fastest growing sector of the pharmaceutical market, now making up about one-third of its total sales.[11]

What has happened to man or culture in the past generation to account for this spectacular increase in medically prescribed psychotropic drugs? Is life more unbearable in the second half of the twentieth century than it was previously? Has contemporary man lost sight of natural, non-medical ways of finding tranquility? Or is it that drug technologies are overprescribed and overconsumed simply because they are available in virtually unlimited quantities?

One important change that is characteristic of contemporary man involves his fundamental attitudes toward life and pain. The Greeks viewed pain as the soul's experience of evolution. The soul-body unity that Aristotle postulated made the body's experience of pain as natural as the soul's experience of knowledge and joy. The Stoics fully acknowledged pain as an irremovable aspect of an irreparably impaired universe. Pain was natural, not evil, and reason mandated tranquil acceptance of the universe as it is. Cicero's teacher Posidonius epitomized the Stoic's acceptance of pain when he said: "Do your worst, pain, do your worst: you will never compel me to acknowledge that you are an evil."[12] Jews and Christians saw pain as purgative and purifying. Christians in particular saw life as a "way of the Cross" and the world as a "vale of tears." Pain was a natural part of life or it had the personal meaning. Some pain could be removed, other pain could be alleviated, but some pain would always remain as a permanent feature of the human condition. The one attitude that is foreign, at least to the classical European tradition, is that pain should be—ideally *always*—destroyed by the intervention of a pharmacist or physician.

Modern man began to lose appreciation for pain's natural, cosmic, and personal meanings with the dawn of modern science in the seventeenth century. At that time Descartes, the father of modern philosophy, introduced a view of man in which man was divorced from the concrete world of matter. The more man saw himself as alienated from a world of matter, the more pain seemed unnatural to him. Cartesian dualism separated man as a thinking thing from the body as a mechanical thing. Pain, therefore, was an indication of a mechanical breakdown, a dysfunction correctible by technology.[13] A new sensibility began to emerge which saw pain as a technologically eradicable evil and progress as the continuing reduction of the sum of human suffering.

Yet a conflict perdures between systems of meaning that are still connected with the classical European tradition and systems of technique which are connected with modern science and its radical dualism. Patients commonly refer to their pain or disease as an "it", an intrusive object, rather than as a characteristic of self.[14] They tend to see their problem as physiological, located within the body, and therefore assume that it can be easily eliminated through chemical therapy.[15] By interpreting their problems in these narrow terms, however, patients can effectively foreclose other levels of intervention. A pain that is symptomatic of a problem that centers on the meaning of life will not be eliminated or resolved through chemical treatment.

Medical civilization tends to treat pain as a purely technical problem and in so doing deprives the patient of discerning the inherent meaning of personal suffering. The experience of pain evokes in the patient fundamental questions such as "Why must I suffer?", "Why is there pain?" or "is my pain telling me something about my conduct or my life?" An attitude that is absolutely set against all pain smothers questions such as these, thereby leaving in oblivion important inquiries and potentially beneficial answers. This is not to imply that tranquilizers and other drugs that affect the central nervous system do not have any legitimate medical use. The point here is that man is not a solitary being self- enclosed in an alien body mechanism. Man is a unitary composite of soul and body, psyche and soma. Pain is not always reducible to a body breakdown or chemical imbalance. Pain may very well have its origin in the kind of personal crisis psychiatrist Viktor Frankl refers to as an "existential vacuum".[16] For many patients the conflict between systems of techniques and systems of meaning is very real. For those caught in this conflict, tranquility cannot be recovered through tranquilizers.

Ironically, as history shows, the more strongly people believe that pain is unnecessary and curable, the more they find it intolerable. For if pain has no meaning, there is no reason it should be tolerated. As Nietzsche has said, what makes suffering so unendurable is not the pain so much as the senselessness of it. We have now reached the point in our society where contemporary man believes he not only has a right but an obligation not to feel pain, tension, anxiety, or stress.[17] Commercial advertising continually reminds him of his right to a "carefree" life and his social obligation to overcome "problem perspiration", "static cling", unsightly dandruff", "ring around the collar", and the "heartbreak of psoriasis". A "Care-Free Travel Plan" assures him that he need not worry about his loved ones being victims of traffic accidents while on vacation, as long as they have sufficient medical insurance. "Extra Strength Excedrin" claims that "Life Got Tougher", so "We Got Stronger", while "New Extra-Strength Tylenol" boasts of being "the pain reliever that's not a hard pill to swallow." Viktor Frankl points out that "it is a well-known empirical fact that in times of war and crises the number of suicides decreases." In the context of a war or a personal crisis, pain and suffering are bearable because the goals that motivate people—victory, saving loved ones, and so on—are the objects of strong and healthy passions, that are more powerful than pain. In periods of peace and prosperity, on the other hand, the removal of pain may be a person's most important goal. Canada's suicide rate for the young has almost quadrupled since the 1950's; the United States rate tripled between 1955 and 1975; in West Germany the number of suicides among the young doubled between 1966 and 1976; and in Japan the rate for suicides of children under 19 has increased by 15 percent since 1977.[18]

A number of scientific studies have borne out the fact that pain tolerance can be greater in times of unusual high stress. Of a group of soldiers severely wounded in various battles in the Second World War, only a third complained of enough pain to require morphine. After the war, of a group of civilians who suffered similar wounds that were surgically induced, 80 percent requested morphine.[19] Virtually all researchers in the phenomenon of pain agree that a patient's attitude toward pain is highly influenced by his culture. Traditional Western culture has interpreted pain as a challenge that has its purpose in eliciting positive, soul-creating responses from individuals. In this sense Keats writes: "Do you not see how necessary a World of Pains and troubles is to school an Intelligence and make it a soul? A place where the heart must feel and suffer in a thousand diverse ways. . . . As various as the Lives of Men are—so various become their souls, and thus does God make individual beings."[20] Today, however, people place extraordinary demands on their economy to have their pain removed promptly and expediently. Thus, the modern trend is for people not to integrate their pain into the general meaning of life, but to depend on the medical profession and the economy to provide them with a life of uninterrupted comfort.

The present overconsumption of tranquilizers, then, occurs not because people need them so much as cultural assumptions lead people to thinking they do. This being the case, people unwittingly allow the medical profession to compromise its ethics as a helping profession to accommodate a new function as a managerial one. What is at stake— more fundamentally than the integrity of the medical profession—is the autonomy of the individual. Peter Schrage warns that slowly and subtly, "science" is repealing the Consttitution and that in the long run individuals "will no longer know, or care, whether they are being served or controlled."[21] Ivan Illich laments the "medicalization of life", and the medical profession's expropriation of man's coping abilities.[22]

Advertisements for tranquilizing drugs that appear in medical and psychiatric journals offer remedies not only for well-established categories of mental illnesses, but for a long list of problems which, until recently, have never been regarded as illnesses. A popular theme in these ads is the housewife who is plagued by nothing more than the usual round of domestic chores. She is often depicted standing in front of stacks of dirty dishes or behind mops and brooms. "Women are impossible," states one ad. "You can't set her free but you can help her feel less anxious." Another ad reads, "Restless and irritable, she growls at her husband. How can this shrew be tamed?"[23] Serentil, a major tranquilizer, is suggested for "the woman who can't get along with her new daughter-in-law." Librium is suggested for the anxious coed for whom "exposure to new friends and other influences may force her to reevaluate herself and her goals."

Roughly two-thirds of the minor tranquilizers are consumed by women, among whom the heaviest users are unemployed domestic housewives, a fact that has aroused the indignation of a number of women's groups. One study reveals that some physicians are more inclined to prescribe drugs to the housewife because they believe she can sleep and does not have to be mentally alert. And if the housewife can resist the negative depictions toward her that appear in the medical profession's ads and attitudes, she still has the subtle pressure of the media to contend with. The Rolling Stones laud the benefits of minor tranquilizers in their song "Mother's Little Helper":

> Doctor please get me some of these—
> And it gets her on her way
> Gets her through her busy day.

Contemporary man's lack of autonomy and his unhealthy and unnecessary dependence on the medical profession is summed up by public health physician Herbert Ratner in the following passage included in a lecture he prepared for a state medical school:

> Modern man ends up a vitamin taking, antacid-consuming, barbiturate-sedated, aspirin-alleviated, benzedrine-stimulated, psychosomatically despoiled animal; nature's highest product turns out be a fatigued, peptic-ulcerated, tense, headachy, overstimulated, neurotic, tonsilless creature.

On previewing these words, a former medical school dean advised Dr. Ratner not to use them: "It will antagonize the drug houses, and we are trying to build up research funds."[24]

Man's passive attitude toward drugs is a reflection of his passive attitude toward life. The net result is a profound insensitivity to both himself and his surrounding world.

> With rising levels of induced insensitivity to pain, the capacity to experience the simple joys and pleasures of life has equally declined. Increasingly stronger stimuli are needed to provide people in an anesthetic society with any sense of being alive. Drugs, violence, and horror turn into increasingly powerful stimuli that can still elicit an experience of self. Widespread anesthesia increases the demand for excitation by noise, speed, violence—no matter how destructive.[25]

Anesthesia and violence go hand in hand. The search for tranquility—in the negative sense of anesthesia—terminates in the discovery of death. This is not a cruel joke played by a deceitful God, but the logical and inevitable working out of a natural law. If man's primary concern in life is to eliminate pain, his preoccupation with the negative leads to more negatives until there is no more life. Pain is an ineradicable part of the human condition. One may eliminate a particular pain, but another pain is always there to take its place. Particular pains may be removed but not pain itself. Peter Schrage remarks that "beyond the Valium is the breakdown, and beyond the breakdown the Thorazine, the hospital, and the shock treatments."[26] If one wants to face life, one must learn to live with pain. Contemporary man, however, has chosen to flee pain rather than face it and in so doing has forfeited the feeling of being in tensely alive.

Tranquility, in the positive sense, is not something one finds by employing a specific technique or by following a particular strategy. It is a quality of the whole person which one experiences as deeply as his life is lived wholly. If one is to find tranquility, he should forget about it and try to live as a whole person. Only then will he find it. Frankl believes that "the present increasing tendency to become addicted to tranquilizing drugs is a sign that contemporary man has been more and more seduced to a belief in the illusion that he can strive for happiness, or for peace of mind."[27] Tranquility, like happiness, is something that happens (the words "happiness" and "happy" are derived from the word "happen"). Tranquility does not result from a motive but arises as a consequence; it must always remain a side-effect and is spoiled to the degree it is made a goal in itself.

Social psychologist Gordon Allport finds that "As the focus of striving shifts from the conflict to selfless goals, the life as a whole becomes sounder."[28] This statement is in accord with Frankl's general theory of logotherapy which holds that man finds the will to live and endure even extraordinary hardships when his life has meaning, an attitude that is reflected in Nietzsche's dictum, "He who has a *why* to live can bear with almost any how."[29]

Frankl discusses the case of a woman who came to his clinic after an attempt at suicide. The woman had just suffered the loss of her eleven year old son; her remaining boy was crippled by infantile paralysis and could be moved around only in a wheelchair. She could not overcome the loss of her son and tried to end her life, but it was her crippled son who prevented her. For him life had remained meaningful, but for his mother it had not. When Dr. Frankl asked the woman to imagine herself looking back on her life from her death bed at age eighty, she suddenly saw meaning in her life, especially in helping her crippled son and sparing him life in an institution. She could now accept her suffering because the life meaning she now found included her suffering.[30]

One must find meaning in his life in order to preserve his tranquility. And he must find meaning in spite of what Frankl calls "the tragic triad of human existence; namely, pain, death, and guilt."[31] This triad brings one face to face with the reality of his human condition. Pain and suffering are inevitable because man has a body and a soul. Death and guilt are also inevitable since man is mortal and fallible. There is no way except through illusion and anesthesia that man can avoid consciousness of these implications of his being.

Edith Hamilton remarks that "it is by our power to suffer, above all, that we are of more value than sparrows."[32] Eugene Kennedy states that, "there is a place for the experience of pain, not for its own sake but because it burns the dross of a man in a way that nothing else can."[33] Human excellence is not achieved through avoiding the inevitable. Man is not free to exempt himself from the human condition; he is free only in how he chooses to stand in the face of the inevitable. Because man can suffer and comprehend the meaning of his suffering, he is of greater value than sparrows. Because he can find meaning in his situation, he can transcend it. Only in this stance can he possess the "peace that passeth understanding."

The contemporary hegemony of the medical profession has narrowed the concept of health to mean medical health. Yet health has an incomparably richer meaning. It is infinitely more than the body's physiological balance. Animal health has little in common with human health. Lobotomized patients still perceive pain but they have lost their capacity to suffer from it; they "adjust", as psychiatrist Thomas Szasz says, "at the level of domestic invalids or household pets."[34] Can we say that they are healthy in the fullest sense of the term? Etymologically, the word "health" is derived from "whole". Health, in its fullest sense, includes man's capacity to deal positively and creatively with the tragic implications of his being. A healthy man is able to accept discomfort, disease, and death insofar as they are unavoidable aspects of human existence. Man's ability to be responsible and human in the face of hardships—something he will not learn from the medical profession—is an essential part of his health. There is a skill to the art of suffering. Ivan Illich writes: "Man's consciously lived fragility, individuality, and relatedness make the experience of pain, sickness, and of death an integral part of his life. The ability to cope with this trio autonomously is fundamental to his health."[35]

The search for tranquility through tranquilizers carries one into the very heart of the anesthetic society. There, one not only tries to feel no pain, but also tries to numb his consciousness to fundamental realities such as self, others, and the basic meaning of his life. A Toronto general practitioner writes: "These are tough economic times, and the reality is you have to work and make money. If giving a guy some pills will help him do it, I will."[36] This kind of advice typifies the anesthetic society's need to reduce reality to a manageable economic machine, a need that is uncomfortably reminiscent of the anti-utopian vision of Aldous Huxley which he expressed in 1932 in *Brave New World:* "But industrial civilization is only possible when there's no self-denial. . . . Otherwise the wheels stop turning. . . . You can't have a lasting civilization without plenty of pleasant vices."[37]

The tranquility that is worth having cannot be the object of a search. It is a quality of man's wholeness and is possessed to the degree man is whole. This wholeness is also a sign of man's health, reflecting his ability to cope with the unavoidable aspects of human existence that are represented by discomfort, disease, and death. Only through self-less and self-forgetful dedication to his authentic vocation and mission in life does man recover himself, his wholeness, his health, and his tranquility.

NOTES

[1] Alfred North Whitehead, *Adventures of Ideas* (New York: The Free Press, 1967), p. 285.

[2] Whitehead, p. 285.

[3] William Wordsworth, "Preface to the Second Edition (1800) of 'Lyrical Ballads'," *College Book of English Literature*, ed. J.E. Tobin, V.M. Hamm, and W.H. Hines (New York: American Book Co., 1949), p. 690.

[4] Edna St. Vincent Millay, "On Hearing a Symphony of Beethoven," *Modern American Poetry*, ed. Louis Untermeyer (New York: Harcourt, Brace & World, 1958), p. 448.

[5] St. Augustine, *City of God*, XIX, 13; trans. Dods, "Peace between man and man is well-ordered concord. . . . The peace of all things is the tranquility of order."

[6] Peter Schrag, *Mind Control* (New York: Pantheon, 1978), pp. 34-5. See the *National Prescription Audit for 1975* (Ambler, Pa.: IMS America Ltd., 1976).

[7] Schrag, p. 136.

[8] Sheila Gormely, "Tranquilizers: The New, Approved Opiate of the People," *Macleans's*, March 22, 1976, p. 58.

[9] Ivan Illich, *Limits to Medicine* (Toronto: McClelland & Stewart Ltd., 1976), pp. 70-1.

[10] Neville Doherty, "Excess Profits in the Drug Industry and their Effect on

Consumer Expenditures," Inquiry X, Sept. 1973, pp. 19-30.

[11]Illich, p. 69.

[12]quoted by Herschel Baker, *The Image of Man* (New York: Harper & Row, 1961), p. 77.

[13]Illich, pp. 147-151.

[14]Eric Cassell, "Disease as an 'It': Concepts of Disease Revealed by Patient's Presentation of Symptoms," *Social Science and Medicine*, 10: 143-6.

[15]Michale Radelet, *Medical Hegemony as Social Control: the Use of Tranquilizers*, Working Paper #135, Institute for the Study of Social Change, Purdue University, May 1977, p. 3.

[16]Viktor Frankl, *Psychotherapy and Existentialism: Selected Papers on Logotherapy* (New York: Simon & Schuster, 1967), p. 17.

[17]Schrag, p. 137.

[18]Frankl, p. 116. Psychiatrist Dr. Harvey Golembek recently stated that in the present peaceful, affluent times about 60,000 high school students in metropolitan Toronto consider suicide each year. See Jane O'Hara, "Young Suicides," *Maclean's* July 30, 1979, p. 20.

[19]H.K. Beecher, *Measurement of Subjective Responses: Quantitative Effects of Drugs* (New York: Oxford University Press, 1959).

[20]John Keats, *Letters,* ed. M.B. Forman (New York: Oxford University Press, 1935), ppp. 335-6.

[21]Schrag, p. 255. Peter Manning with Martine Zucker, *The Sociology of Mental Health and Illness* (Indianapolis: Bobbs-Merrill, 1976), p. 8. "In Western societies, the growth of medicine has enabled it to obtain a powerful hegemony of control over the meanings of 'deviant behavior' and deviance has been seen increasingly as a medical problem." See also Radelet, p. 7. "Because of the lack of power of potentially competing systems of meaning, this hegemony remains fundamentally unchallenged."

[22]Illich, pp. 271-275. "Medicalization constitutes a prolific bureaucratic program based on the denial of each man's need to deal with pain, sickness, and death." p. 131.

[23]Robert Seidenberg, "Drug Advertising and Perception of Mental Illness," *Mental Hygiene* 55, no. 1, Jan 1971, pp. 21-31.

[24]Herbert Ratner, "Medicine: An Interview by Donald McDonald," *Child & Family*, Vol 11, No. 4, p. 366.

[25]Ilich, p. 152. "Pain has become a political issue which gives rise to a snowballing demand on the part of anesthesia consumers for artificially induced insensibility, unawareness, and even unconciousness." p. 135. See also Rollo May, *Love and Will* (New York: Norton, 1969), p. 30. "Violence is the ultimate destructive substitute which surges to fill the vacuum where there is no relatedness."

[26]Schrag, p. 146.

[27]Frankl, p. 41.

[28] Gordon, Allport, *The Individual and His Religion* (New York: The Macmillan Co., 1956), p. 95.

[29]Viktor Frankl, *Man's Search for Meaning* (New York: Washington Square Press, 1966), p. xiii.

[30]Frankl, 1967, pp. 26-7.

[31]Frankl, 1967, p. 15.

[32]Edith Hamilton, *The Greek Way to Western Civilization* (New York: Mentor Books, 1948), p. 168.

[33]Eugene Kennedy, *The Pain of Being Human* (Garden City: Doubleday, 1974), p. 232.

[34]See Thomas Szasz, "The Psychology of Persistent Pain: A Portrait of l'Homme Doulereux," ed. A. Soulairac, J. Cahn, and J. Charpentier, *Pain*, Proceedings of the International Symposium Organized by the Laboratory of Psycholphysiology, Faculty of Sciences, Paris, April 11-13, 1967 (New York: Academic Press, 1968).

[35]Illich, p. 275.

[36]Gormely, p. 58

[37]Aldous Huxley, *Brave New World* (New York: Time Inc. Book Division, 1963), p. 207.

4.
The Person and the Exclusion of Imperfection

The philosophy of the age of enlightenment finally led to the Europe of the black-out.

—Albert Camus

In one of Nathaniel Hawthorne's stories, *The Birthmark*, there is a scene in which Alymer first mentions his wife's defect to her: He asks Georgiana if it had ever occurred to her to have the mark upon her cheek removed. "No, indeed," she said, but perceiving the seriousness of her husband's manner, offered that since it had so often been called a charm, she was simple enough to have imagined it might be so. Alymer, however, pressed his point by declaring that even the slightest defect in his wife was enough to "shock" him, "as being the visible mark of earthly imperfection." The remark angered his wife at first, but then bursting into tears she exclaimed: "Then why did you take me from my mother's side? You cannot love what shocks you!"[1]

Alymer and his wife bring to mind the only two ways in which the problem of love and personal imperfection can ultimately be resolved. Alymer suggests the view that in an ideal world no one would be imperfect and therefore personal love would be unnecessary; Georgiana suggests the view that in an ideal world every person would be loved and therefore imperfection would not matter. Such views differ as much as atheistic humanism does from Christianity. Nonetheless, our world and, indeed, our own lives display a subtle and paradoxical blend of both these views.

Man desires the perfect, and yet must dwell in a world where everything he encounters is imperfect. His love for his fellow man, therefore, is always an occasion of profound conflict since, on the one hand, it aspires to ideal perfection, and on the other, it must serve individuals who are visibly imperfect. "The thing of it is," wrote Montaigne, "we must live with the living."[2] But man does not bear this conflict easily and sometimes tries to resolve it in ways that are dangerous not only to himself but to mankind in general.

Ideals are delightful to imagine and their entertainment never costs anything; it is the encounter with the concrete that always proves resisting and burdensome. Thus, man is perennially tempted to withdraw his love for the concrete, individual person and direct it solely toward the ideal. This temptation is especially powerful in our time because modern technology and utopian-minded planners offer the suggestion that an ideal society of unblemished people is realizable. Yet the ideal without the concrete, the perfect apart from the imperfect, are mere abstractions and exist only in the mind. Remaining faithful to the ideal while abandoning the individual—the preference for aesthetic idealism over concrete realism—provides the basis for what may very well be the most pernicious philosophy of life that man has ever conceived.

The French existentialist philosopher, Gabriel Marcel—who firmly believed that man's essential obligation to his fellow man is concrete, caritative love—appraised his life work "as a persistent, unceasing fight against the spirit of abstraction,"[3] and maintained that "the philosopher can help man to save man from himself only by a pitiless and unwearying denunciation of the spirit of abstraction."[4]

Marcel also believed that a natural and logical connection exists between the spirit of abstraction and mass violence. For, if man is primarily concerned about a perfect order that does not exist, it is inevitable that he come to disdain the imperfect one that does.

Bertrand Russell exemplifies this preference for the abstract in his *Mysticism and Logic* when he states:

> Real life is, to most men, a long second-best, a perpetual compromise between the ideal and the possible; but the world of pure reason knows no compromise, no practical limitation. . . . Remote from human passions, remote even from the pitiful facts of nature, the generations have gradually created an ordered cosmos where pure thought can dwell

> as in its natural home, and where one, at least, of our nobler impulses
> can escape from the dreary exile of the actual world.[5]

It is consistent with man's paradoxical nature that following one of his "nobler impulses"—pure thought or pure reason—he would come not to embrace, but to despise the real world and, along with it, all its real inhabitants. The world of pure reason is probably the world of pure Hell. Robert Frost was fond of "tripping" his friends by stating that the perfect opposite of utopia is not Hell, but civilization.[6]

Syndicated columnist George Will has contrasted the "abstractness" of the political world of Washington with the concreteness of the Christian world of Mother Teresa. Washington is a city that effaces all individual men by having them swallowed up into large categories. The latter is a triumph over the human tendency toward abstractedness; it deals with the crushingly particular experiences of crushed people, one at a time. "It is extraordinary," Will writes, pressing his belief in the natural superiority of the particular man to the political machine, "how extraordinary the ordinary person is."

Without love and good will toward individuals, man's purely rational resources—knowledge, science, technology—serve only to make him more miserable. Reason itself cannot tolerate imperfection and would much prefer ideal possibility to imperfect actuality. To the committed rationalist, therefore, caritative love is an obstacle to progress. The true rational progressivist must anesthetize himself to the plight of the individual while keeping his eye fixed on larger societal goods. Russell expresses in his *Scientific Outlook* how little significance the individual has when viewed from a purely rational-scientific perspective:

> The new ethic which is gradually growing in connection with scientific technique will have its eye upon society rather than upon the individual. . . . We view a human body as a whole, and if, for example, it is necessary to amputate a limb we do not consider it necessary to prove first that the limb is wicked. We consider the good of the whole body a quite sufficient argument. Similarly the man who thinks of society as a whole, will sacrifice a member of society for the good of the whole, without much consideration for that individual's welfare.[7]

In this false analogy, Russell views individuals as organs of the state and disdains acknowledging their true, scientific status as organisms, that is, as living entities that have an autonomy of their own. Consequently, he regards society *unscientifically*, not as a fellowship of many human organisms (or individual persons) but as a single organism of many biological parts. Furthermore, the good of society is the common good, that is, the good of *all* its citizens. Russell's view is not only unscientific, it is unhistoric. The ancient Spartans believed they could improve their society by killing off all children they deemed not strong enough to be Spartans. Yet a careful look at the historical record reveals that not only did the Spartans fail miserably in establishing a better society, but they failed to produce a single outstanding figure in any of the arts, and evolved so enfeebled a society that even to this day it is joked about throughout all of Greece.

It is characteristic of hard, rational thinking not to be deflected by human sympathy. Love for the individual is presumed to be a sentimental indulgence that can interefere with the greater good of society. Yet even if an ideal, rational society were realized, would it be a human society if the individuals who composed it were not loved? If people are desirable because they are perfect, are they not still empty if their existence is not affirmed through love?

Only abstract humans can do without love. The mind alone is sufficient to sustain them. But real, individual people, no matter how extraordinary they are, need more than to be admired for their qualities or welcomed because they fit a social slot—they need to be loved for themselves. Qualities and performances, however perfect or flawless, still remain outside the core of an individual's being. Unless that innermost core is affirmed through love, the individual as such remains unknown and is condemned to a life of alienation.

As soon as something is brought into existence it immediately assumes the stain of imperfection that characterizes all finite beings. Only the abstract retains its ideality, its immunity to imperfection, criticism and rejection. Loveless rationalism is fastidiousness taken to the extreme of fearing actual existence. Frederick Windsor parodies the modern preference for thought over reality in his book *The Space Child's Mother Goose* when he writes: "I have a pet hen whose name is Probable. She lays eggs in concept, being a sophist-bird. But not in reality at all; those would be inferior eggs; for thought is superior to reality."[8] But preference for though over reality proves, in the end, to be a choice for non-existence. Ultimately, as sociologist Daniel Bell points out, "the end process of rationalism is nihilism".[9]

Alexander Solzhenitsyn in *The Gulag Archipelago* comments on the mentality of the Soviet court after the Revolution. "People are not people," he writes, "but 'carriers of ideas'." "And it must also be kept in mind that it was not what he had done that constituted the defendant's burden, but what he *might* do if he were not shot now."[10]

We recall the common place argument that approves abortion on the grounds of what problems the child *might* bring to society in the years ahead. Thus, abortion is sanctioned for sociological reasons. The concrete reality of the child is offset by the hypothetical problems he may cause. Fear of future possibilities precipitates a rejection of present actualities.

Throughout the political writings of Jacques Maritain, time and again, he comes back to his basic premise: that man does not exist for the state, the state exists for man. It is the individual as person who is substantially real and deserving of being accorded dignity and rights. The state as such, conceived apart from the dignity of individual men, is a dangerous abstraction; and the painful tragedy of this spirit of abstraction is that real men are killed for the sake of an empty idea.

Thus Maritain could lament that in the modern world, "Human Reason lost its grasp of Being, and became available only for the mathematical reading of sensory phenomena, and for the building up of corresponding material techniques—a field in which any absolute reality, any absolute truth, and any absolute value is of course forbidden."[11]

By the spirit of abstraction, some desirable quality or factor is separated from the original and total human reality—such as beauty, intelligence, gender, wantedness. Next, that quality or factor, although now existing in an abstract state, is given primacy so that an individual human being—the unborn child, in the case of abortion—may be sacrificed whenever he fails to embody it to a satisfactory degree. Hence, the abstract idea is upheld when often the life of the child is destroyed.

Perhaps no single American novelist saw more clearly the dangers of abstraction than William Faulkner. In 1939 he published two novels, under the collective title of *The Wild Palms*. They were released in counterpoint form: one chapter of 'The Wild Palms" followed by a chapter of "Old Man", then a second chapter of "The Wild Palms" followed by a second chapter of "Old Man", and so on. The effect Faulkner intended was to contrast vividly two types of men: the modern society man and the man of nature.

In the first work, an intern runs away with a married woman who has two children. She becomes pregnant with his child and asks him to abort her. He is reluctant at first but finally consents. In the second novel, a convict serving a life sentence is ordered to rescue a pregnant woman who is a victim of the great Mississippi River Flood. He finds the woman, helps her to dry ground and assists in the delivery of her child.

The irony is obvious. The intern, taught and trained to assist in life, performs an abortion. The life convict, supposedly socially incorrigible, assists in the birth of life. Yet Faulkner is implying more than just society's inversion of life values. In contrast to the natural response of the convict and the woman to elemental conditions of human life, Harry and Charlotte—the central figures of "The Wild Palms"—dedicate themselves to an ideal, a mere abstraction. They isolate love from marriage, children, society, and responsibility; and treat it as if it were an entity unto itself. They flee from family and society to a mine in Utah where, ironically enough, the forty-degree-below-zero cold and the presence of their companion keep them apart for six weeks. When they are finally alone, the cold bursts Charlotte's douche bag—the perfect symbol of nonfunctional love—and she becomes pregnant. Abortion is the logical consequence of their abstracted love.

Faulkner is alluding to the tragedy of modern culture that has lost sight of its proper relationship with nature and reality, that has falsified values by abstracting them from their substance and normal functioning. Charlotte remains dedicated to love but not to her lover, or her family, or the natural consequence of her sexual love, her unborn child. She remains to the end dedicated to love as a free and simple abstract ideal. She dies of a bungled abortion; Harry is subsequently imprisoned for the deed.

The collective desire to pursue an abstraction that all would enjoy is the essential dynamic of utopianism. The Spanish existentialist Ortega y Gasset remarks that "An idea framed without any other object than that of perfecting it as an idea, however it may conflict with reality, is precisely what is called utopia." The utopian dreamer dissolves the natural relationships things have with each other and the moral responsibilities people have for each other. He believes he can have life in terms that are solely his own, devoid of effort, pain, and inconvenience. Yet the realization of such a utopia must produce even more misery than ordinary human existene imposes on us, as Schopenhauer explains:

> Imagine this race transported to a Utopia where everything grows of its own accord and turkeys fly around ready-roasted, where lovers find one another without any difficulty: in such a place some men would die of boredom or hang themselves, some would fight and kill one another, and thus they would create for themselves more suffering than nature inflicts on them as it is. Thus for a race such as this, no form of existence is suitable other than the one it already possesses.[12]

In the imperfect cosmos that we inhabit, a perfect world is not possible. All achievement must be relative, that is to say, we can improve our world but we cannot perfect it. Thus, rather than sacrifice real human beings, in whatever stage of development, for an end that is unattainable, prudence and justice demand that we direct our good deeds on the small, concrete plane of individual people where good can be effectively realized. Modern man's ambitious plans to cure the world inevitably fail because they miss the mark. What is most urgently and immediately needed is the loving care that flows from person to person. Dag Hammarskjold, in his *Markings*, offers these thoughts:

> The 'great' commitment all too easily obscures the 'little' one. But without the humility and warmth which you have to develop in your relations to the few with whom you are personally invovled, you will never be able to do anything for the many. Without them, you will live in a world of abstractions, where your solipsism, your greed for power, and your death-wish lack the one opponent which is stronger than they—love . . . . It is better for the health of the soul to make one man good than 'to sacrifice oneself for mankind'.[13]

Love from the individual, caritative love, involves descent: descent into the suffering world which agonizes in darkness. Love for the ideal, the Platonic form of love, moves in the opposite direction toward the perfect.

A recent statement made by 215 American specialists in ethics, religion, and related fields advised that "abortion may in some instances be the most loving act possible." It is difficult to interpret this form of love for the fetus as anything but a love for the ideal. For it is a love which maintains that any unborn child who cannot attain a certain standard of perfection should be destroyed. But this is not the love that affirms him in his being, that acknowledges and promotes the dignity he possesses as a concrete, living, unrepeatable human.

The absolute disparity of these two attitudes toward love was revealed with dramatic clarity in 1976 as the result of an accident that took place in the town of Seveso, Italy. In July of that year a factory mishap caused four pounds of Dioxin, a chemical agent known as a possible cause of birth defects, to escape into the air of Seveso. Pro-abortionists lost no time in predicting severe deformity for the unborn and advised pregnant women to abort. In all, thirty-six women underwent abortion. Subsequently, five Italian and two German doctors studied thirty-four of the aborted infants and found that in no case could gross or conspicuous malformation be detected.

For what reason, then, did these unborn children die? C.S. Lewis concluded a celebrated trilogy with the admonition: "You will have no more dreams. Have children instead."[14] Were the Seveso abortions done for a dream—a dream of a perfect child or a perfect society? Some women reported being pressured, particularly by feminists, to abort. One, who later gave birth to a healthy son, disclosed that she was urged to abort so as to "help the cause of the abortion bill in parliament." "But," as she explained, "we really wanted the baby."

The debate between the quality of life ethic and the sanctity of life ethic devolves upon one ethic centered on abstractions and another centered on being. According to the sanctity of life ethic, one has a right to be because he is. According to the other view, one may not have a right to be, in spite of the fact that he is, because he is not what he cannot be. The quality of life ethic, in order to approve abortion, must redefine "human" as well as "life". A human is not simply a human but a human with certain perfections. Likewise, life is not life but a certain quality of life. Thus abortion is approved because a given unborn child does not meet standards of humanness and life that exist in the minds of the abortionists. Such is their tendency to regard abstractions as weightier than being.

There is tacit agreement among those who advocate the quality of life ethic that their own quality of life is sufficiently high to justify their own existence. Their function is to pass judgment on the quality of life of others. There is more than a hint of Narcissism here. And we may well wonder whether the world can tolerate an increase of Narcissism. The quality of life vs. sanctity of life debate also turns on the opposition between power and reverence. Those who are willing to judge who shall live and who shall die desire to gain power over the lives of others. Those who uphold the sanctity of life have reverence for all life and ask but to be its ministers.

In a world that already suffers acutely from violence, countenancing such activities as widespread abortion gives this human evil an even firmer foothold. The more afflicted the world becomes, the more anxious it is to change everything at once, and the more willing it is to make sacrifices in the form of human lives for a utopian end state. Yet, in order to effect the change that is most needed, it is, as Hammarskjold has reminded us, the "small" commitment that is needed most.

Mass violence and the spirit of destruction go hand in hand. This is a paradox in that violence is always directed against the concrete. However, it is a paradox based on the essential paradox of man as an imperfect being who seeks perfection in an imperfect world. In his zeal to engineer a perfect society, man employs violence against those whom he regards as obstacles to the attainment of that society, his fellow man, only to emphasize all the more the stigma that has haunted him from his inception: *"Homo homini, lupus est."* Man's moral task, then, is to combine an aspiration for the perfect with a love for the individual. The tragedy of the modern era is that while man has been drawn to the utopian dream, he has remained asleep to the real, concrete needs of the individual person.

NOTES

[1] Quoted by Flannery O'Connor in *Mystery and Manners* (New York: Farrar, Straus, & Giroux, 1980), p. 216.

[2] Quoted by Marshall McLuhan and Quentin Fiore in *The Medium is the Massage* (New York: Bantam, 1967), p. 96.

[3] Gabriel Marcel, *Man Against Mass Society* (Chicago: Regnery, 1962), p. 1.

[4] Marcel, p. 273.

[5] Bertrand Russell, *Mysticism and Logic* (Garden City: Doubleday, 1957), p. 57-58.

[6] See Peter J. Stanlis, "Robert Frost: The Individual and Society," *The In-*

tercollegiate Review, Vol. 8, No. 5, Summer, 1973, p. 228.

[7]Bertrand Russell, *The Scientific Outlook* (New York: Norton, 1962), pp. 223-235.

[8]Frederick Winsor, *The Space Child's Mother Goose* (New York: Simon and Schuster, 1972).

[9]Daniel Bell, *The Cultural Contradictions of Capitalism* (New York: Basic Books, 1976), p. 4. See also Miguel de Unamuno, *The Tragic Sense of Life*, tr. J. Flitch (New York: Dover, 1954): ". . . all which is vital is antirational, not merely irrational, and all which is rational, antivital. And this is the basis of the tragic sense of life."

[10]Alexander Solzhenitsyn, *The Gulag Archipelago* (New York: Harper & Row, 1973), pp. 308-309.

[11]Jacques Maritain, *The Range of Reason* (New York: Scribner, 1952), p. 186.

[12]Arthur Schopenhauer, "On the Suffering of the World," in *The Meaning of Life*, ed. by S. Sanders and D. Cheney (Englewood Cliffs, New Jersey: Prentice-Hall), p. 27.

[13]Dag Hammarskjold, *Markings*, tr. by L. Sjoberg and W.H. Auden (New York: Knopf, 1964), p. 133.

[14]C.S. Lewis, *That Hideous Strength* (New York: Macmillan, 1972), p. 380. See also John Powell, S.J., *Abortion: the Silent Holocaust* (Argus Communications: Allen, Texas, 1981), p. 138: Commenting on the pervasive influence of the mass media, many scientists, the United States judicial system, and other contemporary forces that want to replace a world of care for real people with a world of carefree dreams, Fr. Powell writes: "The euphemisms and the propaganda are like a sweet mask of anesthesia, dulling our sensitivities to the killing, focusing our eyes on the dangling delights of a pain-free world of perfect people."

5.
Life and the Evasion
of Difficulty

And I have asked to be
Where no storms come,
Where the green swell is in
the havens dumb,
And out of the swing of the sea.

—G.M. Hopkins

A few years ago when Birthright held its annual international convention on the spacious campus of Toronto's New York University, several other organizations were holding conventions there at the same time. As a consequence, many participants, feeling like lost freshmen on orientation day, would wander into alien convention areas where they would meet and amiably converse with delegates from other conventions. On one occasion, a group of Birthright women found themselves comparing notes with a group of men who were inadvertent fugitives from a mathematics gathering.

The ladies explained their work in helping pregnant and distressed women. But the men were incredulous. They had no personal experience of unpaid volunteers helping others out of a loving concern that was not in some way grounded in self-interest. In this world, the men insisted, expressing their unquestioned allegiance to the prevailing ethos of the world, "nobody gives anything without expecting something in return." There was obviously something wrong with the Birthright formula, they felt; the equation of give and take did not balance. As the discussion continued, however, the mathematicians began to soften their reluctance to believe, and honestly began wondering whether the testimony of their chance companions—that rare value of "x" for which the men knew no precedent—might actually be true.

The contrast between these mathematicians—spokesmen for rational and worldly values—and the Birthright women—spokeswomen for a more Christian vision—is dramatic and revealing. For it symbolizes the larger and eternal conflict between the ethics of rational self-interest and that of self-forgetful love.

To the strictly rational mind which demands clear and logical explanations of all things, nothing truly extraordinary is ever supposed to happen. There are no miracles, heroes, or even acts of generosity. There is a reason for everything and everything has its reason. Love may be disguised self-interest or merely a glandular condition, but it cannot be a willingness to make personal sacrifice for others—for that is contrary to the symmetry of give and take that reason demands. The equation must always balance. Reason demands reasons for doing things and giving without expecting anything in return does not seem reasonable.

It is easy to understand, therefore, that the most honored laws of the current avatar of rationality—modern science—are models of the most prosaically conservative thinking. The law of the conservation of mass, for example, states that the total amount of mass in the universe remains perpetually the same: nothing can change mass into something which is not mass, nothing can change what is not mass into something which is mass. Mass can neither be created nor destroyed. After any change the amount of mass before and after the change is exactly the same. The right and left hand sides of the equation are always identical. A strictly rational interpretation of the physical universe, therefore, fails to provide any foundation for the plausibility of such Christian acts as love and forgiveness, since love disregards one side of the equation while forgiveness cancels out the other. The rationalistic mind applied to life, then, is at enmity with the Christian outlook.

If we take the rational perspective too seriously we run a strong risk of falling into a sterile cynicism: All human beings are motivated by rational self-interest; people will not work unless they are paid; organizations that do not honor the rational maxims of the world will wither and perish. According to the same rational perspective: Unwanted pregnancies lead to unwanted children and unwanted children invariably produce a myriad of irresolvable social problems.

Yet Birthright and all other charitable organizations that share a Christian vision persist in countering the rationalist's rule. They persist in believing in the unpredictable, the atypical, the revolutionary. In their perspective, hope replaces law because extraordinary things are always possible, and surprise replaces the impassive reception of what is expected because extraordinary things are always happening. Emily Dickinson reflects this attitude of openness when she writes:

> I dwell in possibility,
> A fairer house than prose,
> More numerous of windows,
> Superior—for doors.[1]

Those who make a religion of self-interest inhabit a small and stifling world of measured probabilities and limited expectations. The Christian, on the other hand, who has broken free of the enslaving business of balancing equations, sees a world that is miraculously rich in possibility. It has been said of Emily Dickinson, a recluse from the world, that she who contained a universe did not need the approbation of the secular world. By the same token, the Christian does not need the approval of the secular world because he is alive to realities that transcend it.

Among the highest triumphs of the rational mind is a mathematical formulation scientists refer to as "The Second Law of Thermodynamics" or, as it is sometimes called, the "Law of Entropy." Scientists regard this law as virtually sacrosanct because it represents the most accurate, reliable, confirmable, and majestic scientific statement that has ever been made about the physical world. The great mathematician-astronomer Sir Arthur Eddington states that it holds "the supreme position among the laws of Nature."[2] Lincoln Barnett, in his book *The Universe and Dr. Einstein*, says that it is "the principal pillar of classical physics left intact by the march of science."[3] The law states, in effect, that our physical universe moves just one way: downwards. Energy is constantly being dissipated and as a result, the amount of disorganization in the universe is always increasing. As the sun, for example, sends its energy into space in a random fashion, it is burning itself out and at the same time adding to the amount of disorganization in the universe. In time, the sun and all other energy sources will expire and the universe will be reduced to a state of cosmic death. At this time there will be no life, no light, no heat, no motion—nothing but perpetual and irrevocable stillness.

It is an odd feature of the modern world that educated men still look to science for hope and inspiration.

The great and somewhat embarrassing exception, of course, for the supporters of the Law of Entropy is the advent and evolution of life. How can life be building up, becoming more organized in a world whose most sacrosanct law requires everything to be breaking down, becoming more disorganized? The scientific mind is helpless to explain this rather spectacular exception. It is as if scientists had "proven" that all oranges are perfectly round and were at a loss to explain why not a single orange actually is. At any rate, some scientists regard life as an anomaly that will soon be re-absorbed by inanimate matter. Physicist Sir James Jeans has described the situation imaginatively, though pessimistically: "If the inanimate universe moves in the direction we suppose, biological evolution moves like a sailor who runs up the rigging in a sinking ship."[4]

The rational mind loves uniformity, clarity, simplicity, and predictability. Consequently, all rational laws are idealizations. These idealizations resemble the world just enough to make them credible, but deviate from it just enough to make them false. The rationalist, having observed, for example, that the human body has two arms, legs, eyes, ears, nostrils, lungs, kidneys, and so on, would be tempted to define its organization in terms of the "law of bilateral symmetry" until, at the last moment, he might notice a critical exception—the heart, which is single and situated off-line. But if he ignores the heart to preserve the simplicity of his "law", he allows a rational generality to obscure a hidden truth. As Chesterton says: "Everywhere is this element of the quiet and incalculable. It escapes the rationalists, but it never escapes till the last moment."[5]

The real insight into the world opens our minds to its hidden secrets and suprises that contradict rational regulations. The rationality of the world—like the roundness of the orange—is obvious; its irrationality (call it, perhaps, its "deeper rationality") is more subtle. The world is really a trap for logicians: rational enough to seduce the best of them, irrational enough to prove them wrong. And it is precisely because the rational mind cannot account for everything that Christianity is plausible.

There is a counterpart to the Law of Entropy in the moral domain experienced by those worldly individuals who try to live strictly according to rational self-interest. To their dismay, the longer their life continues, the more difficult it seems to get. Just as the universe is running down physically, their moral universe appears to be running down spiritually. Their acceptance of this "Moral Entropy" is evident in the cynicism they express concerning the possibility of moral growth: withhold contraception from teenagers and they will have unwanted pregnancies; advocate moral values and people will ignore you; be generous to others and they will take advantage of you; help the unwed mother and you will encourage her to have more illegitimate children; support the right of each child to be born and you will add to the population burden. But if moral improvement is impossible, then moral decline is inevitable. And this is the rationalist's dilemma: by being too rational, too preoccupied with self, the law of "Moral Entropy" takes over, causing things steadily to deteriorate.

We find here something psychologically akin to a wearied and demoralized battalion of soldiers that casts aside its arms, abandons its wounded, and spurns relief assistance so that it can devote its remaining energies to retreat. The physical world moves steadily and unerringly toward its dissolution because it can do nothing else; human beings are enticed into following a similar course of dissolution because they deem the alternative to be too difficult. It is much easier to float downstream than it is to battle against the current. What the worldly rationalist does object to is his obligation to accept the conflict he must accept in order to oppose the entropic slide to personal dissolution that threatens to take place within himself.

Yet, the remarkable thing about the physical world is that in spite of pervasive tendencies toward disintegration, life not only exists, but flourishes. Likewise, the remarkable thing about human society is that in spite of pervasive demoralizing forces, goodness and love still abound.

There is a fundamental difference between reason and wisdom: reason sees connections and anticipates what is expected to happen; wisdom is in harmony with higher truths and is open to the advent of something new. Reason deals in simple relationships and cannot account for novelty. Wisdom deals in paradoxes that mirror the infinite.

A California obstetrician by the name of Boyd Cooper has written a book which is a paradigm of rational simplicity—*Sex Without Tears*.[6] Life would be happier and sex always pleasurable, he reasons, if contraceptive and abortion-inducing technologies were universally available and universally accepted. Technology, the practical arm of science, presumably has the power to eliminate difficulty and offer man sex without tears and life without worry.

There is no wisdom in Dr. Cooper's prescription, however, because it contains very little realism. Dr. Cooper's bromide for living is really formulated in a mood of despair. He does not believe in virtue, grace, self-control, wisdom, or morality. Thus, he advises people to give up fighting against the flow of moral entropy. He does not seem to mind that by prescribing a life without difficulty he is actually discouraging people from choosing the only kind of life that is worth living. Without the conflict brought about by death and difficulty, we cannot be saved from our own moral equivalent of cosmic death.

The doctor's prescription needs an antidote, which Emily Dickinson provides in symbolic form:

A Death blow is a Life blow to Some
Who till they died, did not alive become—
Who had they lived, had died but when
They died, Vitality begun.[7]

The courage that is needed to stand against the tendencies toward moral dissolution—love of life and a readiness to accept death—seem, to the rationalistic mind, to be self-contradictory. The rational solution, then, is to find a single, unambiguous virtue by which one retreats from both life and death—to love life less and to be less ready to accept death. The result is a severely attenuated courage which merely seeks to make life less dramatic and death more remote. Such comfortable courage has become immensely popular among today's worldly people, as have other similar "virtues:" average temperance, selective justice, flexible fidelity, optional kindness, and moderate zeal. But the Christian solution is to accept the conflict, the passionate love of life *and* the furious indifference to death. The Christian, as Chesterton once said, "must desire life like water and yet drink death like wine."[8]

Paradoxically, then, self-forgetfulness leads to self-possession, while self-centeredness leads to self-dissolution. Self-possession is achieved and self-dissolution is avoided only by a gesture that is incomprehensible to the rationalistic mind—the uncontradictory clash of two impetuous passions. Psychoanalyst Karl Menninger explains it this way:

> Narcissism chokes and smothers the ego it aims to protect—just as winter protection applied to a rosebud, if left on too late in the Spring prevents the roses from developing properly, or even from growing at all. Thus again psychoanalytic science comes to the support of an intuitive observation of a great religious leader who said, "He who seeketh his own life shall lose it but whosoever loseth his life for my sake shall find it."[9]

Faced with the problem of choosing between unwanted acts (such as abortion) or unwanted people (such as the unwanted unborn), the rationalistic mind chooses the former because it promises to make things easier all around. The Christian, however, chooses the unwanted people because he loves them and at the same time welcomes the difficulties their saving creates. Thus, by keeping two seemingly contradictory virtues separate—love of life and the readiness to accept death (in the form of extraordinary difficulties)—the Christian maintains their mutual health; whereas the rationalistic mind, by mixing the two virtues together, produces a dilution which is no longer really a virtue but a mixture that is too tepid for the rigors of life—the pink that is the blend of red and white. The Christian saves the child and accepts the difficulties. The rationalistic mind is disinclined to do either.

Rational self-interest invariably leads to a diminishing of love for others and an intensifying of one's fear of difficulties. Philosopher Ayn Rand writes in her book, *The Virtue of Selfishness*, that "the actor must always be the beneficiary of his action and that man must act for his own *rational* self-interest."[10] What Miss Rand seems not to realize, however, is that rational self-interest is too paltry an ethic to make its practitioner a beneficiary. As the Christian knows so well, the human person transcends both rationality and self-interest: through life and death his destiny and the destiny of others are mysteriously intermingled. Consider these lines from the poet John Masefield:

> In the dark womb where I began
> My mother's life made me a man.
> Through all the months of human birth

Her beauty fed my common earth.
I cannot see, nor breathe, nor stir,
But through the death of some of her.[11]

Nonetheless, we observe in our worldly society the undeniable evidence of diminishing love for others and increasing fear of death. There is, on the one hand, the decline in love we read in the escalating rates of abortion, child battering, spouse battering, divorce, homicide, rape, kidnapping, and terrorism. On the other hand, there is the terror of death that expresses itself in the vain attempts to escape it through speed, noise, drugs, alcohol, sex, youth worship, and innumerable other ways. Yet the truth remains: we preserve our passion for life only by maintaining our willingness to accept death.

In no way do we mean to underestimate the magnitude of our present difficulties. Two points, however, should be stressed. In the practical expression of personal, self-forgetful love, difficulties often function to elicit a purer love. By maintaining our courage in the face of difficulties, our love will stand to grow stronger. Secondly, if difficulties prove too much for one person, it may simply mean that an organization of people dedicated to loving others in a self-forgetful way must come into existence. Throughout history, in times when it seemed that personal and social problems were too formidable to be redressed, religious orders came into being which repeatedly showed the world that there is greater power in devotion to life than exists among the dark, disorganizing forces of the underworld; that love, in the final analysis, is more practical and realistic than despair.

The welfare of human beings is too important to be abandoned because of the prospective difficulties involved. Today people are on the verge of forgetting what extraordinary effort is required to keep the human race together. Instead of keeping their love and courage vital so they can counter the difficulties that oppress them, they lapse into a dangerous moral inertia and quote cynical maxims about how everybody is out for themselves and how it does not pay to help one's neighbor. They are strongly tempted to believe that technology can do everything for them, thereby obviating the need for them to do anything for themselves. Ironically, the moral death effected by moral inertia is destructive; whereas the death to one's fear of difficulties and the dying to one's rational self-interest are liberating.

The ancient Greeks had two radically different notions of life: *psyche*, which means individual life in the biological and psychological sense; *zoe* which refers to the Life we all share, the unending Life of God. Rational self-interest knows only the first meaning of life. The Christian knows the second. In this sense Life is greater than any of us, though it includes us. Those who protest: "It is my life, I can do with it as I please," betray a lack of awareness of its sacred and transcendental reality.

These two meanings of life, though distinct, represent realities that are in continuity with each other. We live, biologically and psychologically, as individuals. At the same time we participate, through our individual lives, in a universal life that is their source and destination. The continuity between *psyche* and *zoe* is repeatedly expressed in diverse ways as the universal testimony of mankind: "Life is a flame that is always burning itself out but catches fire again every time a child is born" (George Bernard Shaw); "A baby is God's opinion that the world should go on" (Carl Sandburg); "Every child comes with the message that God is not discouraged of man" (Rabindranath Tagore).

The larger purpose of our life is to live not only for something that transcends it, but for someone who will outlast it. When we defend the whole of Life—even where it is manifested in but a single, individual life—we begin to experience the whole of Life. Here is the final and decisive repudiation of the mathematician's equation applied to life. The rational mind's equation of *quid pro quo* excludes Life. The tragic fate of the individual who lives rationalistically and exclusively for himself is to be ever haunted by a sense of his own approaching death. In a purely rational perspective, an individual's gradual and inevitable decline is merely one small illustration of the realization of that intractable force, canonized as the law of Entropy, by which the entire physical universe moves steadily and irresistibly to its death.

North Sea fishermen who wanted to keep herring alive and fresh until they returned to port learned through experience that captured herring quickly die if they are separated from another fish which is their natural enemy. The enemy fish provided a vital stimulus that the herring could not live without. Difficulty, even in the form of persecution, can be beneficial in supplying a needed spark of life. For this reason, St. Ignatius prayed that his Jesuits would always be persecuted.

The Christian may not always welcome difficulty with the same enthusiasm as an Ignatius of Loyola. Nonetheless, he should at least know that since life and difficulty are inseparable, two distinct virtues are necessary: one to affirm life and another to face difficulty. And he should also know that in order to keep each of these virtues strong and serviceable, he must not compromise them, as does the rationalistic mind, producing a weak amalgam that can only unite him with the downward drift of the cosmos. Rather, he should keep his virtues vigorous by accepting the conflict that life and difficulty naturally present.

NOTES

[1] Emily Dickinson, *Complete Poems of Emily Dickinson*, ed. by Thomas H. Johnson (Boston: Little, Brown & Co., 1960).

[2] Sir Arthur Eddington, *The Nature of the Physical World* (Ann Arbor: University of Michigan Press, 1958), p. 74.

[3] Lincoln Barnett, *The Universe and Dr. Einstein* (New York: William Morrow, 1966), p. 103.

[4] Sir James Jeans in *Eos*, quoted by Dorothy Sayers in *The Mind of the Maker* (London: Methuen & Co., 1959), p. 112.

[5] Chesterton, *Orthodoxy*, p. 81.

[6] Boyd Cooper, *Sex without Tears* (New York: Bantam, 1972).

[7] Dickinson, *Complete Poems*.

[8] Chesterton, p. 93.

[9] Karl Menninger, *Man Against Himself* (New York: Harcourt, Brace & World, 1938), pp. 381-2.

[10] Ayn Rand, *The Virtue of Selfishness* (New York: The New American Library, 1964, p. x.

[11] John Masefield, *Poems*. Collected edition in 1 volume (New York: Macmillan, 1953).

6.
Freedom and the Renunciation of Restriction

It should not be surprising that a revolt is occurring against the mores which people think cause alienation; a defiance of social norms which promise virtue without trying, sex without risk, wisdom without struggle, luxury without effort. . . .

—Rollo May

As soon as one begins to talk about the foundation of morality he is immediately confronted with two major difficulties. First, his language and imagery will inevitably appear idealistic to some, making him vulnerable to the criticism that he is calling for a mode of human comportment that is unattainable and consequently unrealistic. Second, as he expounds on morality's "do's" and "don'ts", he will be accused of being dogmatic. Those who view morality in this reactionary way— as fanciful idealism set to impersonal dogma—will turn to a morality of their own, usually one that is woven around their own desires.

The so called new morality is supposedly purged of any traces of idealism or dogmatism. It is alleged to be a morality of freedom since it centers around one's own desires rather than someone else's rules. Yet it is a deception. People are not morally free simply because they can do as they desire. For desire itself is grounded in unfreedom. If one acts only according to his own desires, he is a slave to his own appetite. Such a state, slavery in actuality, is an immoral state. The free man must sacrifice his unfree will that is controlled by things and instincts so that he can exercise his free will through which he chooses his proper destiny.

In practice, of course, no one seriously and consistently advocates a morality of pure desire. A student may extol radical libertarian views for himself, but insists that his examiner be a paragon of fairness. A pornographer or a drug pusher may preach "do your own thing", but both are highly moralistic when it comes to getting the market value for their wares. There is honor even among thieves. The essence of morality of desire, then, is simply making a moral exception of oneself. In this regard, it is incompatible with the Golden Rule of "doing unto others what you would have them do unto you", which remains the one moral precept common to all history's viable moral philosophies.

Hamlet says of man:

> What a piece of work is man! how noble in reason! how infinite in faculty! in form and in action how like an angel! in apprehension how like a god! the beauty of the world! the paragon of animals![1]

In so describing man, is Hamlet guilty of idealistic nonsense? Hamlet is reminding man of his great dignity, and his extraordinary potentialities. Such apparent idealism is actually indispensable in urging man toward human and moral excellence, for reminding him of his noble endowment and high calling. Man needs inspiration which serves as an antidote to the rigors of life that can easily discourage him. Robert Browning's image that man's reach should exceed his grasp is not intended to promote frustration but to indicate that man's proper trajectory in life is always upward.

On the other hand, consider the behaviorist B. F. Skinner's assessment:

> To man *qua* man we readily say good riddance. "How like a god!" said Hamlet. Pavlov, the behavioral scientist, emphasized, "How like a dog!" That was a step forward.[2]

Is this realism? Or is it man's death warrant as human, his tacit acceptance of regression to the sub-human state? "Man," writes Ortega y Gasset, arguing in behalf of man's rightful destiny, "is the being condemned to translate necessity into freedom."[3]

Moral idealism is not unrealistic as long as it is grounded in man's truth, in his real capabilities. At the same time, the rules of morality are not necessarily impersonal. In fact, they help to insure that man's moral conception of life transcends egoism. Rules help to civilize man, make him aware of the need for reciprocity, of fairness in his dealings with other persons. Encouraging the adoption of moral virtues such as justice, courage, temperance, prudence, veracity, and unselfishness is not unrealistic. What is unrealistic is the belief that society could hold together in the absence of these virtues.

Man is a moral being because he is unfinished and stands in an ambiguous relationship with his destiny. Hence Man's moral nature is the key to understanding the dramatic character of human existence. To choose morally means to affirm, in the face of conflicting pressures, one's true self, and thereby to will the emergence of that self.

Man is a temporal creature who faces backwards and forwards in time, drawing strength from the past and growing in hope toward the future. But he is also a creature of space, looking inward and outward, affirming his inner self as well as his fellow man. He lives not only by reason but by love. And it is the warmth of his love that assures him that ideals are not unrealistic and rules are not mere dogma. He chooses to remain free and continually to resist conformity to some abstract norm or conventional image.

He chooses the more difficult paths: excellence rather than mediocrity, freedom rather than slavery, authenticity rather than adaptation, truth rather than illusion. To be moral, then, is to choose for oneself what no one else can choose for him—to be oneself.

The foundation of morality, then, is man in his elementary condition as he faces four directions in time and space, having the power to know and to choose the larger reality of who he is. The following passage from Robert Bolt's *A Man for All Seasons* illustrates this point. While Thomas More held firm to his moral convictions, less courageous men were, from personal interest, siding with King Henry VIII. In one scene, More quarrels with the Duke of Norfolk and says to him:

> And what would you do with a water spaniel that was afraid of water? You'd hang it! Well, as a spaniel is to water, so is a man to his own self. I will not give in because I oppose it—I do—not my pride, not my spleen, nor any other of my appetites but I do—I![4]

More then goes up to Norfolk and feels him up and down and asks "Is there no single sinew in the midst of this that serves no appetite of Norfolk's but is, just Norfolk? There is! give *that* some exercise, my lord!"

The indispensable value of courage to society is underscored by Alexander Solzhenitsyn in his 1978 address to Harvard University's graduating class: "A decline in courage may be the most striking feature which an outside observer notices in the West. . . . Such a decline in courage is particularly noticeable among the ruling groups and the intellectual elite, causing an impression of loss of courage by the entire society. . . . Should one point out that from ancient times a decline in courage has been considered the beginning of the end?"[5]

The basis of morality can be expressed in more metaphysical language. Man always *is* more than he appears to be. The reason for this is that his being unfolds in time. Moreover, his being properly does so only as he freely chooses it to do so. Man's essence (what he is in a perfected way) and his existence (what he actually is at any given moment) are not in perfect accord. A moral good, then, is what brings man's essence and existence into greater unity; a moral evil is what further divides them from each other. The courage to be, then, is the will to exist in accordance with one's essence.

Man's proper destiny is to choose in the direction of actualizing his potential, of becoming more and more the human being he ought to be. Christian philosophers have always emphasized the importance of human will—*voluntas*—in the evolution of the moral person. Ortega y Gasset, writing of the modern absence of will, coins the term *noluntas*, as the negative freedom of will by which man turns away from his true destiny.[6]

The true foundation of morality may appear tenuous to someone who prefers his morality to be supported by the masses or verified by science. In contrast to being faithful to oneself, that is, to something that is historically unprecedented, one might find the beaten path more reassuring or find more comfort in conformity. Yet, in the end, evading the moral self for the approval of the masses or the security of material things proves fatal. When the separation of man's existential life and his essential destiny reaches a critical distance, he can no longer hold himself together and death ensues. The West has lost its will to live, argue some social critics. Malcolm Muggeridge sees the contemporary acquiescence to ease, literally, as a choice for death:

It is difficult to resist the conclusion that Western man, wearied of the struggle, has decided to abolish himself. Creating boredom out of affluence, impotence out of his own erotomania, vulnerability out of his own strength, he himself blows the trumpet that brings the walls of his city tumbling down. Until at last, having educated himself into imbecility, and drugged and polluted himself into stupefaction, he keels over, a weary, battered old brontosaurus, and becomes extinct.[7]

If the foundation of morality seems too tenuous, thus causing considerable apprehension, then an authentic life would seem too dangerous. Hence it is common for man to avoid a true moral life for himself while being content to observe a fictionalized form of it acted out by others. Thus, the importance of media heroes: movie stars and sports superstars, for example. Here, the individual who struggles in the face of danger and against great odds to achieve, is considered not an idealist but an idol. A star hitter stands at home plate with a slender cylindrical bat gripped tightly in his hands hoping to hit a small spherical object darting toward him at a speed approximately one hundred miles an hour, between agile fielders who stand poised, ready to thwart that hope. He succeeds but slightly more often than three out of every ten times at bat, and yet is a hero and commands a salary several times that of the president of his country.

Rather than participate in life, many are content to observe a fictionalized representation of it. In the case of professional sports on television we have the curious phenomenon of international audiences numbering in the millions regularly watching the image of a man playing at the image of life. As Ortega observes in *The Revolt of the Masses*, "The mass-man will not plant his foot on the immovably firm ground of his destiny, he prefers a fictitious existence suspended in air."[8] We see this peculiar form of self-alienation reflected in sundry examples of contemporary folk humor and literature: "I get up in the morning, read the obituary column and if my name isn't there I celebrate by taking a drink and going back to bed." "Is the world so visibly degenerating or is the news coverage just getting better?" Anthony Burgess has Alex, the protagonist in his novel, *A Clockwork Orange* say: "It's funny how the colors of the real world only seem really real when you viddy them on the screen."[9] Walker Percy's title character, Lancelot, makes the observation that " . . . the movie folk were trafficking in illusions in a real world but the real world thought that its reality could only be found in illusions. Two sets of maniacs."[10]

Nature does not complete man; nor does science, politics, higher education, culture, or the entertainment industry. Man completes himself through his own struggle, one that proceeds from a basis in moral freedom and aspires to a realization of himself and no one else. And, although this struggle does not go on without the help of others, it is always the self who is at the center of his developing life.

Wisdom, according to the ancient Greek philosophers, is communion with reality, and is achieved through a long apprenticeship in knowledge, self-discipline and virtue. But the value of a wise man is not confined to himself. Because reality is the measure of wisdom, the wise man has something real to offer others in his community. Moral evolution is never a private affair. The Greeks, fathers of moral philosophy, had no word in their vocabulary to express 'private morality'. Man is a self, but he is also a social animal and grows simultaneously as an individual and as a responsible member of his society.

An individual, however, who has little knowledge, self-discipline, and virtue is not, by himself, in a favorable position to grow morally. He needs the wisdom that someone else has; and the relationship of one who lacks wisdom to one who possesses it is that of a disciple to an authority. The function of authority in a community, then, is to help guide others to their proper destiny. Therefore, authority is harmonious with individual freedom. Jacques Maritain states that " . . . authority and liberty are twin sisters who cannot do without each other, and authority in some is *for* liberty in others."[11] Furthermore, the nature of a political community requires that there be men in authority in order to bring about the good of the community. Authority is not an imposition but a necessity.

Popular intelligence, however, takes pleasure in opposing things that are in reality complementary. Authority is therefore commonly regarded as an opponent of liberty rather than an assistant in its development. There are no philosophical reasons for holding such a view; however, there are historical and political ones.

In the usual functioning of authority, there is the accompaniment of power in order that the right of authority, that is, the right to be listened to or obeyed, is secured. However, not everyone who is in a position of authority acts in a manner that is worthy of his position; some use authority merely as a pretext for the exercise of power. Paul Tillich distinguishes between "authority in principle", which can be exercised unjustly, and "authority in fact,"[12] which has an inherent claim in justice, In short, the authoritarian and the authority are not the same. The authoritarian exercises power over people and inhibits their liberty; the authority guides people through his own wisdom in the interest of fostering their liberty. Moreover, even those who are worthy of their office may not always exercise their power correctly; they may err in the practical exercise of their power.

To someone who does not distinguish authoritarian power from rightful authority, or the improper use of authority from its proper use, authority may very well appear incompatible with freedom. Man may even believe that God Himself is an enemy of freedom. Merleau-Ponty, for example, writes: "Moral conscience dies at its first contact with the Absolute."[13] The same position holds for atheistic existentialists who claim that the death of God is the first condition of the liberty of men. In addition, authority and freedom can seem mutually antagonistic to the proud individual who claims that he has already achieved moral perfection and does not need anyone else's counsel, and to the private individual who claims that he should be accountable only to himself.

Moral authority, at times, has existed independently of political power. In fact, moral authority can be all the more striking and effective when it is separated from power, as shown in the case of Christ who is an enduring example of one who retains great moral authority in spite of his having submitted powerlessly to crucifixion. Historically, various judicial bodies from the Roman Senate to the United States Supreme Court have had great authority although they did not exercise power. On the other hand, power cannot be justified if it is separated from authority. The tyrant and the criminal are examples of individuals who exercise power without authority. Consequently, authority is more fundamental than power; it can exist properly by itself, and in conjunction with power it serves as power's justification. Yet power cannot stand by itself nor can it justify authority.

Another source of modern confusion concerning the nature of authority and its proper function is the *Social Contract* of Jean Jacques Rousseau. Rousseau had a considerable influence on the social philosophy of America's Founding Fathers. His influence, strangely enough, has also

been felt among anti-establishment revolutionaries of the nineteen six-
ties who chose to drop out of that same American society. Rousseau
begins his *Social Contract* by stating: "Man is born free; and everywhere
he is in chains"; he proceeds to argue that, "Since no man has a natural
authority over his fellow, each individual should obey only himself."[14]
For Rousseau, equality and authority are incompatible. No man can be
a natural authority over another because everyone is naturally equal.

"Man is born free," Rousseau states. It is the primitive who is morally sound. Knowledge, self-discipline, and virtue are superfluous. Christianity, which comes into conflict with primitive values, does not heighten
moral consciousness, it interferes with it. Man's natural state, of course,
is one of slavery. Moral freedom, if it is to come at all, is achieved only
through struggle—a struggle that is sustained by love, guided by reason,
and endured through virtue. In a certain sense, the contemporary Skin-
nerian behaviorists are the logical descendents of Rousseau, for in treating
everyone as a scientizable atom, the presumption is made that everyone
is the same.

People are equal in the eyes of the law, or equal in their humanity;
but they are not absolutely equal, as any plain girl knows who observes
the popularity of her prettier rival. The worst form of inequality, reasoned
Aristotle, is to try to make unequal things equal. "Equals ought to have
equality," he insisted, and recalled the retort of the lions, in the fable
of Antisthenes, when in the council of the beasts the hares clamored for
equality. "Where are your claws and teeth," asked the lions?

What is missing from Rousseau's philosophy is a notion of
brotherhood. People are neither absolutely equal nor are they totally unequal. They are brothers, which means that they are equally lovable
although sufficiently dissimilar by nature and achievement that one is
entitled to have authority over another. In this way parents can have
authority over their children and teachers over their students without the
humanity of children or students being disparaged in any way.

We have noted that popular intelligence is fond of opposing things
that are, in truth, complementary: "authority and liberty" is one example, "authority and power" is another, "authority and equality" is a
third. This tendency not to see the complementary and life-serving opposites that are harmoniously joined to things represents a failure of the
moral imagination. It is like seeing the paint but not the painting, or liv-

ing life while remaining insensitive to duty. Each reality has its spiritual counterpart which can be discerned only when egoism and materialism have been transcended.

When President Carter presented his eulogy in honor of the late Senator Hubert Humphrey, he cited Mahatma Gandhi's "Seven Sins of the Modern World" and remarked that although the senator had sinned in the eyes of God, as do all humans, he never exemplified any of the sins on Gandhi's list. These sins are not, in themselves, evil so much as they represent a lack of moral vision. They each lack coordination with the spiritual value which is their proper moral complement:

1 Wealth without work
2 Pleasure without conscience
3 Knowledge without character
4 Commerce without morality
5 Science without humility
6 Worship without sacrifice
7 Politics without principle

Altogether, these "Sins of the Modern World" indicate Life without Spirit. But life without a vitalizing spirit soon becomes wearisome. Such a life often occasions men to multiply their acquisitions and intensify their power in an attempt to defeat their discontent. But what man needs is to let go of what he has so that he can gain the vision whereby he can see more clearly the fullness of what is. The Roumanian essayist E. M. Cioran makes the comment that, "So-called civilization teaches us how to take possession of things when it should initiate us in the art of letting go, for there is neither freedom nor 'real life' without an apprenticeship in 'depossession.' "[15]

We return to the point that it is man's proper vocation to be always unfinished, always ascending, always aspiring. The more he develops, the better he understands this. Kierkegaard remarks that maturity consists in realizing that "there comes a critical moment where everything is reversed, after which the point becomes to understand more and more that there is something which cannot be understood." Not only must man's reach exceed his grasp, but as he grows, an ever widening gap appears between them. If he accepts this, he grows in reverence and humility.

It has been said that if a man is not reverent, he become cynical. But the cynic is a de-spiritualized being, suffering, as Oscar Wilde notes, from the perversity of knowing the cost of everything and the value of nothing. Cynicism is the penalty for trying to divorce spirit from life. Thus we come to another brace of ideas which the popular intelligence opposes—growth and humility. It seems foolish, indeed, to the man of the world that the more he grows the smaller he should become in his own estimation. He is conceited, so the phrase goes, but he has good reason to be. Yet the greater the man, the more eager he is to serve; and the wiser he is the more he is willing to submit to authority.

Man has faces in four directions at the same time: outwards and inwards, forwards and backwards. As he deepens his understanding in each of these directions, he deepens his regard for the mystery of things and their natural kinships with the infinite. In this perspective the scope of his own authority appears quite limited. G. K. Chesterton confesses that he is at a loss to understand the Church's enthusiasm for physical virginity. But he is wise and humble enough to consider the terrible disproportion that exists between himself and the world, his own particularity and the Church's universality. And so, he writes:

> With all this human experience, allied with Christian authority, I simply conclude that I am wrong, and the church is right, or rather that I am defective, while the church is universal. It takes all sorts to make a church; she does not ask me to be celibate. But the fact that I have no appreciation of the celibates, I accept like the fact that I have no ear for music. The best human experience is against me, as it is on the subject of Bach. Celibacy is one flower in my father's garden, of which I have not been told the sweet or terrible name. But I may be told it any day.[16]

NOTES

[1]Shakespeare, *Hamlet*, Act II, Scene 2.

[2]Albert H. Hobbes, "Dignity and Degredation," *The Intercollegiate Review*, Vol. 8, No. 5, Summer 1973, p. 243.

[3]José Ortega y Gasset, *Meditations on Quixote* (New York: Norton, 1961).

[4]Robert Bolt, *A Man for All Seasons* (Scarborough, Ontario: Bellhaven House, 1968), p. 72.

[5]Alexander Solzhenitsyn, *A World Split Apart*, an address given at the Harvard Commencement Exercises Thursday, June 8th, 1978, reprinted

by The Wanderer Press, 1978, pp. 4-5.

[6]José Ortega y Gasset, *The Revolt of the Masses* (New York: Norton, 1960), p. 103.

[7]Malcolm Muggeridge, *Christ and the Media* (Grand Rapids, Michigan: Eerdmans, 1977).

[8]José Ortega y Gasset, *The Revolt*, p. 105.

[9]Quoted by Robert Hughes, "The Decor of Tomorrow's Hell," *Time*, December 27, 1971.

[10]Walker Percy, *Lancelot* (New York: Farrar, Straus & Giroux, 1977), p. 152.

[11]Maritain's position on this point is extensively elaborated in *Scholasticism and Politics* (Garden City: Doubleday, 1960); *Man and the State* (Chicago: University of Chicago Press, 1956), and *Du* régime temporel et la liberté (Paris: Desclee de Brouwer, 1933).

[12]Paul Tillich, *Love, Power and Justice* (New York: Oxford University Press, 1969), pp. 89-90.

[13]Quoted by Leon Joseph Cardinal Suenens in *Love and Control* (Westminster, Maryland: The Newman Press, 1961), p. 11.

[14]Jean Jacques Rousseau, "The Social Contract," *Great Political Thinkers* ed. by William Ebenstein (New York: Holt, Rinehart, and Winston, 1965), p. 441.

[15]Quoted by Karl Stern in *Love and Success* (New York: Farrar, Straus and Giroux, 1975), p. 95.

[16]Chesterton, *Orthodoxy*, p. 156.

7.
Marriage and the Rejection of Sacrifice

I fear the barnacle which might latch on and not let go—so I keep my womb empty and full of possibilities.
—Erica Jong *(in a poem)*

In 1976, Ann Landers shocked many of her readers when she announced the results of a survey she had taken. She had asked the parents among her readers to respond to the question, "What would you advise a young couple who is trying to decide whether to have children?" Of the slightly more than 10,000 parents who responded, seventy percent said that if they had it to do over again, they would not have children. Miss Landers herself, as she continues to inform us, is still reeling from shock.

Yet shock is not an altogether appropriate response to the survey's results. Has not the seventies been justly named the "Me Decade"? Has not our own recent historical epoch in a "culture of narcissism" (Christopher Lasch) featured the glorification of the "imperial self" (Quentin Anderson), the absolutization of the "right to privacy" (U.S. Supreme Court's 1973 abortion ruling), and the popularization of "looking out for number one" (the wisdom of best-sellerdom)? And what could be less congruent with the "Me Generation" than accepting the kind of endless sacrifice that is demanded by having and raising children? Still, Ann Landers and many of her readers express surprise, dismay, and even shock over the fact that a majority of parents in a national survey say they would, if they could do it over again, have childless marriages.

It is hardly a national secret that the recent secular religion of self-fulfillment has pushed the traditional notion of sacrifice—especially the kind entailed in rearing children—if not into oblivion, at least into the dark cultural corners of disrepute. In recent years there has appeared a virtual deluge of popular books positively discouraging married couples from having children. First there was Ellen Peck's *The Baby Trap*; then the Silvermans' *The Case Against Having Children*; then Kathrin Perutz's *Marriage is Hell*; and Peck and Sederowitz's *Pronatalism, The Myth of Mom and Apple Pie*. All these works echo the same ideology, namely, that children should be a purely personal choice and that husband and wife should think first and foremost of themselves. Ellen Peck expresses the urgent hope that most married couples avoid having children and that the minority who do, have their children reared by professionals. " . . . it would be wiser," she writes, "to regard parenthood as a specialized occupation—and childlessness as our cultural norm."[1]

The Silvermans add that today's married couple is less eager to have children because "of the many alternatives available for personal fulfillment outside of traditional family life" and the flowering of women's liberation that "not only makes women aware of their options but provides them with the psychological strength to take them." A contributing editor for a national magazine puts the matter more tersely: "rearing children is not sufficiently self-centered to be fashionable."

Surveying the popular women's magazines we find similar examples of anti-natalism. Lynell Michels, writing an article in *Redbook* called "Why We Don't Want Children," states: "All around us, we see young parents struggling with budgets, baby-sitter problems, measles, crayon-marked walls and other assorted annoyances too numerous to mention." N.B.C. Nightly News correspondent Betty Rollins, in a 1970 *Look* article called "Motherhood: Who Needs It?", advises: "It is not a question of whether or not children are sweet and marvelous to have and rear; the question is, even if that's so, whether or not one wants to pay the price for it. . . . If God were still speaking to us . . . even He would probably say, 'Be fruitful. Don't multiply'."

The September 1977 issue of *McCall's* carried a piece entitled: "How Children Can Hurt a Marriage" in which the authors—a man and a woman— state: "Instead of bringing husbands and wives closer together, children often drive them apart by creating new tensions or serving as a battleground for old ones.'' In that same month *Redbook* featured a questionnaire asking: ''How Do You Really Feel About Having Children?'' The word ''really'' in the title subtly implies that today's married couples do not feel as positively disposed toward having children as their ancestors did, an implication made explicit by the editors who state: ''Today as never before, having children is regarded not as a duty but as an option to be freely chosen.'' This exact point is made again two months later in a *McCall's* article, ''Do I Want a Baby?'', whose caption reads: ''Unlike their mothers and grandmothers, today's young women do not see having children as their obligation—or even, necessarily, their goal.''

In general, media propaganda conveys the view that the modern, enlightened couple ought to decide the question of offspring by weighing the self-fulfillment they promise against the self-sacrifice they demand. Inevitably, according to such a cost-benefit analysis, sacrifice is easily envisioned as outweighing fulfillment. Nonetheless, the appropriateness of using this type of calculus is rarely discussed. The underlying assumption, however, is that parents should be primary beneficiaries of their children. Typically, a New York *Times* Book Review article (Nov. 13, 1979) declares that a ''new breed'' of parents are ''in nearly all cases . . . becoming parents because they have chosen to do so, and . . . view the prospect as a challenging and fascinating project.'' Yet we are left to wonder what happens when, after a few years, the challenge and fascination begin to wear off. Do we expect the acceptance of a greater sacrifice than was anticipated? Or do we expect separation and divorce so that the disenchanted parties are free to look elsewhere for new challenges and fascinations? The shortsightedness of the self-fulfillment criterion often proves tragically unfulfilling for the others involved, in particular the children who were conceived and brought into the world primarily to benefit their parents.

The statistics tend to bear out the unpleasant truth that the era that hitched its hopes to a star of self-fulfillment did not succeed in achieving very much self-fulfillment, at least for its married citizenry. Between 1958 and 1974, for example, the divorce rate in the United States rose 150 per cent, with the annual number of divorces climbing to nearly one million. The number of children affected by divorce each year rose from 379,000 in 1957 to 1.1 million in 1974. At the same time the fertility rate (births per 1,000 women aged 15-44) had fallen from 122.7 in 1957 to 66.7 in 1975. During the "Me Decade"'—from 1970-1979—the number of traditional husband-wife families grew at a rate of 6.6 per cent from 448 million to 47.7 million, but the households maintained by women with no husband present increased 51 per cent from 5.5 million to 8.5 million and the number of families maintained by a man without a wife present increased 33.6 per cent from 1.2 million to 1.6 million.

In Canada, more than 10,000 women a year are opting out of their marriages and leaving their children behind. In the 1971 census there were about 25,000 divorced and separated mothers without custody of their children. In the 1976 census the figure rose to 47,000 and by 1979 it was 77,000.

Historian Allan C. Carlson, writing in *The Public Interest* (Winter, 1980), points out that the dominant voices today in sociology and family-counselling professional journals strongly emphasize wide-open choices, experimentation, uninhibited sexuality, and the primacy of self-fulfillment. Concerning the current view of the liberal consensus on self-fulfillment, Carlson writes:

> Morality demands freedom for people to realize their own potentials—and their own needs, desires, and tastes—with a minimum of social rules and regulations. Relationships should last only so long as they are mutually self-fulfilling.

Carlson also points out that the view that couples have a right to remain "childfree" is shifting to questioning whether they have a right to *have* children.

Added to and reinforcing the pro-self-fulfillment and antinatalist propaganda supplied by books, magazines, television, professional counsellors, and professional journals, is that supplied by the federal government. Senator Joseph Tydings, for example, introduced a resolution in the United States Senate calling for America to commit itself to a national goal of zero population growth, arguing that "a growing population makes the solution of nearly all our problems more difficult and more expensive." The Tydings resolution mirrors on a federal level the same reluctance to sacrifice for children that is found on the personal level. If married couples are reluctant to make sacrifices for the children, why should the federal government be any different?

Perhaps the oddest of all the recent political proposals to discourage people from having children (or at least from having more than two children) belongs to Herman E. Daly which he made to the Joint Economic Committee of Congress, chaired by the late Senator Hubert Humphrey, and which appears in the committee's publication, *United States Economic Growth From 1976 to 1986: Prospects, Problems And Patterns.*[2] Daly's proposal calls for "transferrable birth licenses." Each woman, according to the proposal, would receive 22 coupons or "subunits" from the government. If she has a baby, she uses up 10 of these units. If she has another child, she uses another 10 subunits, and is then left with a 2 "deci-child" (two-tenths of a child) remainder. She may sell her last two "deci-children" subunits, trade them, or bequeath them to one of her descendents. On the other hand, she might try to deal with other coupon holders until she has obtained enough coupons to authorize another child.

The coupons would be exchanged on a "free market" basis with appropriate punishments meeted out where an "unlicensed" woman produces an "illegal" child for whom she does not have the requisite 10 coupons. Daly foresees a reduction in the coupon quota when economic pressures and the like force the federal government to adopt a Negative Population Growth which he anticipates would be about 1.8 or 1.9.

The most evident and computable cost in working out the cost-benefit analysis of having a child is economic. Because of the peculiar power to fascinate that figures have—"intoxication is a number," wrote Baudelaire—they are often credited with possessing a reality they really do not have. On the other hand, the possible qualitative benefits of having children cannot be represented by anything as clear, determined, and intoxicating as a number. The usual result is that the quantifiable costs of having children seem much more real than their corresponding qualitative benefits.

Thomas J. Espenshade—working with the Population Reference Bureau, Inc., a Washington educational concern—provides 1980 figures for the projected cost of seeing a child through birth, 18 years under the parental roof, and four years at a public university. He calculates this cost for the middle-income United States family to be $85,000. By including "lost" earnings to a mother who chooses to stay home with her children, the cost climbs to approximately $140,000, up about 30 per cent from 1977.

Thomas Tilling, a contributing editor of *Parents* magazine argues that this $140,000 figure is unrealistically low. Using the federal figures issued by the Agriculture Department as a starting point and accounting for annual inflation (but not counting college), *Parents* arrives at a figure of $254,000. Other estimates for raising a child to the age of 18 are as high as $326,455. States one social critic: "It's the height of irrespon-·sibility to spend that kind of money on something unless you really believe it's a well thought-out investment."

Such calculations, however, are misleading since they do not include tax paid on income against exemption allowances for children. Nor do they take into account an incentive factor which motivates many people who do have children to earn more, behave more responsibly and live longer (and as a result their life-long earning potential). Moreover, they are abstractions and cannot be applied to large groups of people. The average middle-income family cannot save a quarter of a million dollars over a period of eighteen years simply by not having a child. In addition, by abandoning procreation altogether, society would not abound with wealthy childless couples, but be brought to the edge of economic catastrophe due to the massive unemployment effected by the extinction of all child-dependent industries.

The philosopher Hegel remarked that the birth of children is the death of parents. The great American champion of "rugged individualism" and Social Darwinism, William Graham Sumner, stated that "the interest of children and parents are antagonistic. . . . It may well be believed that, if procreation had not been put under the dominion of a great passion, it would have been caused to cease by the burdens it entails."[3] In our own time we are witnessing the increasingly widespread adoption of this view that children are actually bad for a married couple. We may well suppose they are bad if their presence is evaluated against the narrow criterion of parental self-fulfillment ("narcissistic entitlement" as one family expert puts it).

Prior to the White House Conference on the Family that took place in the summer of 1980, the General Mills Corporation circulated to each of the conference delegates the results of an extensive survey the company had done of family members. The survey described the existence of "new-breed parents" who specifically reject the idea of sacrificing for their children. Mention of such parents should not come as a surprise. Three years earlier the highly reputable Berkeley demographer Judith Blake told the nation: "You won't find those sacrificial mothers any more." And a few years earlier than that, Germaine Greer had told her readers that parental sacrifice is a hoax:

> We, the children, who were on the receiving end knew that our mother's self-sacrifice existed mostly in their minds . . . We could see that our mothers black-mailed us with self-sacrifice, even if we did not know whether or not they might have been great opera stars or the toasts of the town if they had not borne us.[4]

Historian James Hitchcock, a governor-appointed delegate to the White House Conference from the state of Missouri, makes the remark that "the now deeply-ingrained expectation of self-gratification virtually in-sures, in many cases, that the spirit of self-sacrifice necessary to all successful relationships cannot be summoned."[5]

The needs of parents and children are not antagonistic to each other. The antagonism that exists between parents and children is, for the most part, the result of parents insisting on maintaining a self-gratification ethic in a situation that demands self-sacrifice. And yet, self-sacrifice is not antagonistic to parental needs.

If we look more closely at people who are used to making sacrifices for others, we notice that they do not regard their sacrifices precisely as *sacrifices*. There is a good reason for this. In a very real and fundamental way, we all need others. The current fashion that urges us to assume an air of self-sufficiency and denigrate needing others does not alter this fact; it merely serves to anesthetize ourselves to a fundamental truth about our human condition. Not to be aware that we indeed do need others is, as C.S. Lewis notes, a "bad spiritual symptom", just as the absence of a feeling of hunger is a bad medical symptom since we do really need food. We need others because we are not self-sufficient and therefore depend on others for what they can give us. But we also need others because we need someone to be the recipients of our gifts. There simply is no other satisfactory use we can make of our talents— indeed, our lives—than by directing them to others. When a person is acutely aware of this radical need to receive from and give to others, and acts accordingly, he does not consider himself to be making sacrifices as such; rather, he considers himself to be living in harmony with his humanity, acutely aware of himself, others, and the natural interdependence that obtains between the two.

Our need, then, is four-fold: We need others to be our recipients and they need us to be their recipients. At the same time, we need others so that we can benefit from what they give, and they need us to benefit from what we give. In the first place, recipients are needed to make giving possible; in the second, beneficiaries are needed to make benefitting actual. Being a recipient fulfills the need in the other to give; being a beneficiary fulfills the need in the self to receive. Since we and others are both givers and receivers, our relationships in fundamental need is four-fold.

Sacrifice, as it is popularly understood, is intelligible as a concept only when it is perceived as incompatible with self-gratification. But, in a deeper sense, a life dedicated to pure self-gratification (self-fulfillment in the narcissistic sense) represents a form of self-sacrifice which, in a peculiar way, outdoes the sacrifice of the saints. For total self-gratification demands the sacrifice of who we really are—human beings who naturally exist in a relationship of four-fold need with others. A life of total commitment to self-gratification represents the total sacrifice of personality—total self-dissolution. Again, the paradox: we reject what seems like death—sacrifice—only to discover that in rejecting sacrifice we welcome death.

The traditional notion of sacrifice—particularly, sacrificing for spouse and children— really means a form of purification in which we sacrifice our illusions for the fuller realization of who we are. The question, then, is what shall we sacrifice: reality for illusion, or illusion for reality?

Parental sacrifice, therefore, is compatible with personal fulfillment in a most profound way. Not only does it provide continuing opportunities to give to and receive from others, but it represents the deepest and most original gift that can be conferred upon another—that of life itself.

Indeed, the needs of parents and children are not antagonistic to each other. In his immortal Dialogue, the *Symposium*, Plato develops the notion that nothing is more natural, spontaneous, and consonant with human needs than to have children, for, as he explains, happiness expresses itself by the desire to reproduce the beautiful. Married couples who are happy, then, will want to have children; and in so doing, will fulfill a natural and human need—the need to reproduce what is beautful and good in themselves, in offspring of their own flesh. We might even call this need "selfish," but it is selfish in a most generous and creative way. Mindful of increasing social pressure not to have children, British novelist Margaret Drabble dared to state a few years ago that her children were her greatest pleasure. In a piece she called "With All My Love," she derided the anti-baby movement and praised that particular form of "selfishness" that is fully compatible with love and sacrifice, and commonly known to us as *parenthood*.

> I have heard from American friends that the anti-baby movement is so well in hand over there that they are surprised to see how openly and proudly baby shops and maternity shops still display their wares over here; perhaps they will end up discreetly in back alleys, where lovecraft used to conceal its offerings . . . It doesn't upset me very much selfishly, because I got my children already; I got them in before it became really disreputable.[6]

The relationship between need and love is a complex one. Love is higher than need, and yet we need to love. While it is true that we stand in a need relationship with others that is four-fold, we would most probably not accept the obligations of such a relationship if we did not transcend our need concerns through love. Without love, entering into even a four-fold need relationship, on the face of it, is indistinguishable from a complicated business arrangement that disguises a root concern for selves. In love, however, we are willing to forget our selves and all our needs, but in our loving others, we begin, though unintentionally, to fulfill our needs.

It is love, then, that allows our sacrifice to seem so natural, so appropriate, that it is virtually unnoticeable. Yet, stated in this manner, the point may seem unduly idealistic. What we want to say is this: our reluctance to make the ordinary sacrifices that are required by our relationships with our spouses and our children has its source in a lack of love. Stated positively: we are willing to make appropriate sacrifices to the degree that we love. In the absence of love, the family withers, disintegrates, and dies.

Herbert Hendin, in his book *The Age of Sensation* (1975), which is based on a psychoanalytic exploration of several hundred college-age people, makes this stark observation:

> The increasing emphasis on solitary gratification and immediate, tangible gain from all relationships only encourages an unwillingness in parents to give of themselves or tolerate the demands of small children. It is not surprising that the family emerges through the eyes of many students as a jail in which everyone is in solitary confinement, trapped within their own particular suffering.[7]

The same disquieting perception of the current state of the family has moved psychiatrist David Cooper to describe the family as the "ultimate perfected form of non-meeting."[8] Hendin defines the generation of young people he studies in terms of "its active pursuit of disengagement, detachment, fragmentation, and emotional numbness." These young perform but do not feel, they indulge in sensory experiences but do not accept emotional involvement. They are not people who give love a prominent place in their lives. In fact, some appear steeled against it. Says one of Hendin's subjects: "My parents aren't the type who sacrifice themselves for their children. I don't think parents should."[9]

Marriage without sacrifice is marriage without love, which in one sense is no marriage at all. Nonetheless such a form of marriage remains popular, no doubt reflecting the equally popular view of life in which the pleasure of self-gratification is severed from the pain of commitment. "Bodies are united by pleasure, but souls are united by pain," wrote the Spanish existentialist philosopher Miguel de Unamuno. By failing to accept the conflict between pleasure and pain, gratification and commitment, one indicates his unreadiness to accept the conflict between marriage and sacrifice.

Midge Decter, speaking at the Harvard Club in New York City (May, 1980), on the present day pathology of being "In Love with the New Sterility," denounced the pervasive attitude that assigns no overriding value to parenthood. According to Miss Decter, we are not witnessing new form of "freedom;" we are suffering acutely from new forms of misery—and misery that is already taking dead aim on despair. For we are presently experiencing:

> a time when strong and handsome prosperous young couples refuse to carry on life by reproducing themselves and instead expend their

capacities for love and care on a ghastly narcissistic attention to self; a time when young women talk endlessly of growth but deny themselves their most important opportunity for widening and deepening and enhancing their lives; a time when young men fear to speak of masculinity in the only terms that make it significant—that is, the protection and support of women and children—and spend their manly energies on the care and beautification of their bodies.[10]

Nicolas Berdyaev has warned the modern world that "If there were no childbearing, sexual union would degenerate into debauchery."[11]

To the individual whose only concern in life is his singularized, atomized self, marriage is indeed perceived as a "trap," as "Hell," as a "jail in which everyone is in solitary confinement", as an occasion for "narcissistic entitlement" and the "worship of sterility". Such a completely unrealistic perception of marriage, however, is rooted in a chronic fear of death. Marriage demands a high degree of personal wholeness; it demands openness to the needs of others; it demands love. Without these indispensable ingredients, the sacrifice it demands does not seem natural and appropriate; it seems deadly.

Because marriage is so intensely realistic, it brings the elements of life and death into disturbingly clear focus. But to those who are not ready for marriage (yet are attracted to the evident "life" implications it promises—pleasure, intimacy, companionship, pooled income, etc.), the death element, particularly in the form of sacrifice, seems too formidable to be endured. Yet death is a dominant feature of marriage. "It is the entire symbolic function of marriage and family," writes Michael Novak, "to remind us that we come from dust and will return to dust."[12] Marriage is dirty dishes and dirty diapers, repairing furniture and repairing feelings, the maintenance of the household and the peace therein, soothing hurts to body and soul, incessant interruptions, inconveniences, intolerances, and incomprehensions. Marriage ought to be disillusioning. It is not a utopian escape from death; yet the "new-breed" of married couples look on it precisely as that.

If there is a Devil, he would surely want us to choose death. But since the Devil is wily, he lures us to death not by praising it, but by playing on our fantasies of a carefree and eternal life which spring from our fear of death. Consider the heroin addict. To subject oneself to heroin is to take flight from the pain of life to a persuasive, though momentary, illusion of immortality. But the laws of the human organism are such that the heroin user needs larger and larger doses of his drug in order to achieve the same fantasy until he comes to the point where he must choose death in the form of an overdose or life in the form of the unillusioned consciousness of his own morality. The Devil would seduce us into marital death not by denouncing the sex act but by promising us pure and ecstatic sexual delights blissfully free from the sacrifice demanded by offspring. But in the end, one must choose between a sterile and meaningless use of sex which portends, in its emptiness, the ruin of one's marriage, and a creative and meaningful use of sex which is open to life and consonant with the norms of a full and generous marriage.

Life without death is our fantasy of life. Likewise, marriage without sacrifice is our fantasy of marriage. Such fantasies are the products of our fear of death. But our fantasies cannot provide us with life; only life can. Our fantasies can provide us only with death. Thus, fear of life can lead straight to death; whereas the acceptance of death through love for life leads to life and life in greater abundance.

Our radical weakness is our reluctance to love, indeed, our fear of love. We are now witnessing a time when popular attitudes toward marriage play to this fear. Yet if love is removed from marriage so that sacrifice does not remain, marriage inexorably becomes a form of death. We are invited to espouse a new form of marriage that promises us *exemption* from the struggle and conflict that sacrifice requires. But that *exemption* is in reality a *deprivation*, for it deprives us of precisely what marriage must be in order for it to carry out its loving and life-incarnating purpose.

NOTES

[1]Ellen Peck, *The Baby Trap* (New York: Pinnacle Books, 1972), p. 20: "I want to tell you about this trap, not because I see babies as the enemies of the human race, really, but because I see babies as the enemies of *you*."

[2]This idea was first put forward by Kenneth Boulding in 1964. Section B of Professor Daly's article, "The Transition to a Steady-State Economy" is reprinted in *The Human Life Review*, Vol. III, No. 2, Spring 1977, pp. 123-125.

[3]William Graham Sumner, *Folkways* (Boston: Ginn, 1906), p. 310.

[4]Germaine Greer, *The Female Eunuch* (London: Paladin, 1970), p. 150.

[5]James Hitchcock, "Family is as Family Does," *The Human Life Review*,

Vol. VI, No. 4, Fall 1980, p. 58.

[6]Margaret Drabble, "With all my Love," Op-Ed page of New York *Times*, August 4, 1973.

[7]Herbert Hendin, *The Age of Sensation* (New York: Norton, 1975), pp. 256-7.

[8]David Cooper, *The Death of the Family* (New York: Random House, 1970), p. 4.

[9]Herbert Hendin, p. 296.

[10]Midge Decter, "The New Sterility," *The Human Life Review*, Vol VI, No 4, Fall 1980, p. 26.

[11]Berdyaev, *The Destiny of Man* p. 242.

[12]Michael Novak, "The Family Out of Favor," *Harper's Magazine*, April, 1976.

8.
The Unborn and the Fear of Finitude

The fear of life is the favorite disease of the twentieth century.

—William Lyon Phelps

The abortion movement over the past few years has expanded its frontiers, promoting live fetal experimentation, infanticide, forcible sterilization, active euthanasia, and even the aborting of certain healthy and wanted children. Moreover, in an attempt to secure the broad institutionalization of its ethical outlook, it has sought vigorously, by various political and non-political means, to exclude its opponents from the democratic process, insisting that neither "private morals" nor "religious dogma" have any valid role to play in shaping public and secular laws. The movement's aggressive advance brings to mind the story of Lincoln's farmer who said: "I'm not greedy about land—I only want what joins mine." Yet the movement is not securing a moral empire for itself. Rather, as John T. Noonan Jr. contends, it is "driven by a deep logic" toward its inevitable self-destruction. Noonan compares it with the slavery movement of the past century whose own excesses brought about its destruction.[1]

What is at the cognitive core of the abortion movement, one might ask, that gives rise to so self-destructive a logic? What is the abortionists' fundamental vision of things? It is, as I will attempt to demonstrate, an inverted way of evaluating the metaphysical reality of human life in which life that *is not* is given greater importance than life that is, in which *possi-*

ble life (life that is not yet, but could be) takes precedence over *actual life* (life that already is, whether pre- or post-natal.) Precisely because the movement gives more weight to *what is not* (possible being), such a radical attachment to the negative must involve it more and more intimately with non-reality, until its own dissolution is finally effected. The essential difference between the pro-abortion movement and its life-affirming counter-movement is that the former is willing to dismiss certain human realities as if they were nothing and value the hypothetical as if it were real, while the latter is committed to affirming all human realities and honoring their primacy over what is not real.

It may be instructive here to recall an experience I had a few years ago as a member of a panel discussion on abortion. The audience was composed chiefly of university students and, keeping their own stated convictions in mind, I had prepared what I believed to be an appropriate strategy. I planned to argue that abortion is a violent way of resolving a human conflict and that, especially where human life is at stake, we should seek to resolve human conflict in more imaginative, more humane, and more peaceful ways. I had not, however, anticipated the kind of strong response this approach would provoke.

The panelists who sat on either side of me were women who had undergone non-therapeutic abortions. Their purpose that evening was to defend abortion as a basic right of women. The woman to my right, confident that a single quotation was sufficient to make her point, was content to do nothing more than read a sentence from an early work of Pierre Trudeau: "Few men are aroused by injustice when they are sure of not being its victims themselves."[2] Her point was that since men cannot become pregnant, they are generally unconcerned about the "injustice" of withholding abortion from women whose unwanted pregnancies are a grave burden. She did not consider the unborn child a pertinent reality. I noted that this argument is actually self-defeating: Many men are concerned about abortion precisely because they stand to be its victims. So often, abortion directly and negatively affects their relationships with the aborting women as well as their own identities as husbands, lovers, fathers, and males. But more importantly, who will be aroused by the injustice that abortion imposes upon the unborn? People who are already born cannot be aborted. *They* do not need to worry about suffering the injustice of being killed in the womb. Hence, if we take seriously Trudeau's cynical remark, women and men would be equally unlikely to be concerned about injustice for the unborn. But such is demonstrably not the case. The pro-life movement does not consist of worried fetuses.

The woman to my left had a more direct way of avoiding the reality of the unborn. She declared herself opposed to violence of any kind, but pleaded that abortion is not an act of violence. "The *real* violence," she said, "is what happens to the child when he is rejected later in life." This was her 'metaphysical' analysis of abortion and her retort to my carefully conceived strategy. She judged potential violence to the child later in life to be real violence and abortion—what I took to be real flesh and blood violence—not to be violence at all. No one contends—I thought to myself, giving the logic of what I had just heard a different application—that poor people should be done away with because the real violence lies in the suffering their continuing poverty might impose on them and not in the acts that would end their lives. The two women opposed me because I was inevitably "unjust" since I could not become pregnant, and "unrealistic" since I was concerned about what is happening to living human beings *now*. I sensed the existence of a new metaphysical outlook on life and wondered how widespread it might be. In a certain sense, my strategy was more successful than I could have imagined because it exposed to many people in the audience whose ethics were still connected to the real world that in order to justify abortion, one must separate him or herself from reality, arguing that possible violence is more real than the violence which ends life.

A short time thereafter I was in Nova Scotia at the Halifax conference on Ethics and Public Policy. The distinguished theologian James Gustafson delivered a paper there in which he defended the rights of human beings not yet conceived to be permitted to fulfill their interests. He implored the present generation not "to deprive future generations of opportunities for well-being."[3] I caught up to him at the coffee break and mentioned his conspicuous avoidance of the rights of those conceived but not yet born. "Can you arouse a genuine interest in the rights of those who do not exist without first establishing the rights of those who do?" I asked. He found my question disagreeable and declined to comment on it. Dr. Gustafson, in his liberality, spoke tenderly of nonhuman forms of life and even described certain inanimate beings as "our neighbors", but it did not seem incongruous to him that the human unborn should remain a uniquely underprivileged class.

At the apogee of a serialized debate in *Newsday* about the comparative values of an unborn human and a budding leaf, Long Island's favorite tabloid printed these words from a Centerport youth: "What right has an unborn human to grow up and destroy the earth that a budding leaf, [which] would contribute to the earth's survival, does not?"[4] Future survival becomes the goal, not present rights; sacrifice today's unborn for tomorrow's leaves and the future of the world! The new metaphysics was definitely alive in the high schools.

In 1970, at "a highly secretive symposium in New York City",[5] Garrett Hardin presented a curious transvaluation: "If the space required to grow four redwood trees could be devoted to growing food for one person, we should say directly and bluntly that four redwood trees are more important than a person." Hardin reasons that "we are guardians of the future." However, with regard to human life, he states: "You can always produce more babies."[6] We are not owners of trees, but presumably we do own babies. The demands of the future are more urgent than those of the present. Babies are not individualized, unrepeatable human beings but faceless members of a species of secondary importance. They are assumed not to have self-hood—one is as good as another—and their existence is subject to revocation on the basis of subhuman and futuristic criteria.

By 1975, Hardin's calculus, which credited four redwoods with a stronger claim to existence than one person, had come to seem tame and unnecesssarily cautious. Now the discontinuation of human life was sanctioned for something far less substantial than trees. *Atlantic* published an article by Willard Gaylin, M.D., and Marc Lappe, Ph.D.—both of the Institute of Society, Ethics, and the Life Sciences at Hastings-on-Hudson—that called for further expansion of the abortion frontier. In the article, the doctors write: "The total destruction of one or two *normal* fetuses to protect against the possible birth of one abnormal fetus, under current law in the United States, is not legally objectionable."[7] That is to say, the lives of some should be discontinued so that the births of some others can be prevented. One does not die so that someone else or even something else might live, but so that another shall not live—the justification of death being to serve the cause of more death.

In more specific terms, with respect to hemophilia, the authors tell us that they not only allow but sometimes encourage the practice of aborting the *normal* male who is virtually indistinguishable from his affected brother. Here they approve abortion to ensure that half the time, a hemophilic person is not brought into the world. Thus, the *normal* dies so that the abnormal will not live; the elimination of one group is justified in terms of guaranteeing the elimination of another. Moreover, the aborted normal males would quite probably be wanted if their true genotype were known. Here, the abortion movement, which was inaugurated by the desire to eliminate the abnormal and the unwanted, is extended to include the normal and the wanted.

In the same article, Gaylin and Lappe call for the legalization of live fetal experimentation. They reason that there can be no valid objection to scientific experimentation on fetuses that are already scheduled for abortion because the knowledge so gained can be of inestimable help to future wanted babies. Of course, in terms of the new metaphysics, in which the possible takes precedence over the actual, they have a point. If society allows a child in the womb to be subjected to "unimaginable acts of violence" such as "dismemberment, salt-induced osmotic shock, or surgical extirpation"[8] how can it balk at fetal experimentation, most forms of which are incomparably more benign? Also, if society removes protection from the unborn whom nature had destined for life, consistency would demand removing protection (for the sake of experimentation) from those unborn whom parents and physicians have condemned to death. If society is to abandon the unborn and commit itself to the future, it should do so with thoroughness and consistency.

By 1978 it was time to put this metaphysical view into the hands of the North American homemaker. In its July issue, *Redbook* featured an article by Margaret Mead entitled "The Many Rights to Life". "Clean air and safe water have become rights to life for all living things," she declares.[9] The venerable sociologist writes warmly and generously about the right to be mourned after death, the right "to vanish into the unremembered past", the right to "decent shelter", and the right to "a chosen sexual identity", but strongly disagrees that there is "the right of the conceived but unborn to emerge alive from the womb."[10] Thus, she opposes what she calls the "absolutism" of the Right to Life Movement and approves amniocentesis followed by abortion so that couples may avoid "the tragedy of having predestined a living being to defective survival."

Dr. Mead does not consider that the right to life, because it is elementary and prototypic, is the right to have other rights. By withholding *this* right all other alleged rights become, at best, mere adjuncts to privilege. If one does not have a right to enter the theater of life, he or she has no claim to the goods that exist therein. Mead's theory of rights makes as much sense as someone making himself the beneficiary of his own will: one cannot be heir to life's fortune if he or she is not first heir to life. Again, as with Gustafson, the whole order of nature is endowed with rights save a single seed—the human unborn.

More recently, in response to a study which revealed that 308 retarded children under 18 years of age were forcibly sterilized in 1976 in Ontario, Canadian Health Minister Dennis Timbrell ordered a nine-month halt to such sterilizations, pending government review of the issue. Mary Van Stolk, national president of the Tree Foundation—a research group that claims to oppose violence in the family and to defend the rights of children—denounced the Health Minister's action. She states: "The focus should not be on the rights of the mentally retarded, but on the rights of the children that would be produced if there were no sterilizations."[11] What Ms. Van Stolk appears to say is that we must deny people their human rights and impose violence on them in order to withhold life from those who do not yet exist. Actual violence in the form of forcible sterilization is not considered to be violence at all in light of the potential violence visited upon hypothetical people in the form of their being allowed to live. Again, in this new metaphysics, the rights of the actual children are ignored while the rights of non-existent children are invoked. And even when these rights *are* invoked, it is in a negative sense: the "right" never to be.

Finally, we note the practice of women aborting because their child is the "wrong sex". In these cases the parents often view procreation as a consummation of a plan rather than as an unconditional gift of life to another. Therefore, the child of undesired sex, though a being that is real, is destroyed because he or she is not the being that was planned. The parents may try again for a child of the "right sex", conferring a greater claim to existence upon that possible child than upon the other.

Once again, the child who does not yet exist is more highly valued than the one who does.

It is easy to imagine a better world; it is another thing to work with the one we have. Human life is the tattered product of a flawed and finite universe. We know too well the thousand ways life may be maimed. In our apprehension we ask: Will the pregnancy displease, upset, shame, or deprive the parents? Will the child be deformed, ill, or unhappy? We see life threatened on all sides and begin to believe that the only sure way to spare it anguish is to destroy it, thereby exemplifying Paul Tillich's description of neurosis as "the way of avoiding nonbeing by avoiding being."[12] The hardships, the negative elements of life, are summarily avoided through avoiding life itself.

Through the prism of fear, nonbeing can seem powerful enough to be more real than the human reality it threatens. Modern existentialist artists have expressed this point often and with dramatic force. The elongated and severely emaciated human figures of the sculptor Alberto Giacometti "seem to be invaded by the surrounding void."[13] Samuel Beckett exclaims: "Nothing is more real than nothing." Ernest Hemingway, in his story "A Clean, Well-Lighted Place," put these words into the mouth of his fearful hero: "Our nada [nothing], who are in nada, nada be thy name . . . ; Hail nothing, full of nothing, nothing is with thee. . . . " These artists are proclaiming that the experience of human finitude is the experience of a seemingly positive, though frightening, nonbeing as a permanent feature of the human condition.

At the same time, the desire for more perfect forms of human life can be so strong that it can mistake an imaginary ideal for something that is real. Here, *what is not*, like a mirage, can assume the shape of *what is*. This confusion is commonly found among Marxist utopianists who place greater value on ideals that do not yet exist (perhaps cannot exist) than on those real human beings who do.

The inverted metaphysics of abortion, then, is rooted in the fear that being will be dissolved by nonbeing. But it is also rooted in a hope that results in an idealization of what might be. Thus, it generates two unrealistic dispositions: one of needless pessimism about the actual world (how free abortionists are with the word 'tragedy'); and one of indefensible optimism about an idealized world (the 'Age of the Wanted Child'). Here the optimism and pessimism are gratuitous because neither is grounded in a realization of *what is*. To the abortionist, the unwanted fetus is unrealistically bad; the unconceived, planned fetus, unrealistically good. What he does not seem willing to accept is the conflict inherent in all real beings. The fetus always partakes of conflicting characteristics: the good and the bad, life and death. Martin Heidegger writes:

> To the opinionated life is only life; death is death and only death. But life's being is also death. Everything that enters into life also begins to die, to go toward its death, and death is at the same time life.[14]

In contrast with abortion's inverted metaphysics is the life-affirming view. In this view *what is*, e.g., the being of the fetus, is affirmed with full acceptance of the uncertainties, difficulties, and various images of nonbeing with which it is inseparably united. Thus, love and courage are essential: love, to affirm what the fetus is; courage, to take on the negatives that every affirmation of being requires. Again, according to Tillich, "Courage is the readiness to take upon oneself negatives, anticipated by fear, for the sake of a fuller positivity."[15] He goes on to explain that without this kind of life-affirmation, life cannot be preserved or increased. He adds that the more vitality a person has, the more he or she is able to affirm life in spite of the dangers announced by fear and anxiety. Conversely, this vitality is lacking in neurotic individuals and in neurotic periods.

The course of action discussed and approved by Gaylin and Lappe in which the normal unborn are occasionally destroyed as a way of insuring the destruction of the hemophilic unborn offers not only a particularly clear example of what Tillich means by avoiding non-being by avoiding being, but an equally clear example of how the abortion mind, impelled by its own relentless logic, is continuously enlarging its circle of victims. On the other hand, if a person reads the testimonies of Robert and Suzanne Massie and their hemophilic son, Bobby, in their book, *Journey*, he or she is struck by the great courage shown by this remarkable family and how, by taking on negatives, one may attain a fuller positivity.

Without courage, love tends to degenerate into sentimental kindness. This seems to be the case in the allusions made by Gustafson and Mead in which inanimate things are considered "our neighbors" and clean air and safe water are "rights to life". The inherent weakness of sentimental kindness is not its lack of benevolence but how it buckles in the face of difficulties. For most people, all that is required to feel kind is that nothing threaten them at that moment. But let a man who is merely kind enter a truly uncomfortable situation and his kindness may quickly give way to cruelty. As C.S. Lewis points out, such "kindness consents very readily to the removal of its object,"[17] for it is concerned not with whether its object is good or bad, lives or dies, but only that it escapes suffering.

Consider, again, Margaret Mead's rhetorical statement that an unborn child who is possibly deformed should be aborted so that his or her parents can avoid "the tragedy of having predestined a living being to defective survival." If we read the obverse of this statement, we find that abortion is "a blessing that prevents a living being from any kind of survival." An act of sentimental kindness can seem appealing when it is described in terms of avoiding pain or escaping suffering, even when that same act is morally reprehensible.

Because love reaches out and affirms the life that is, it may be characterized as a movement toward the real. It is in this sense that the life-affirming attitude is realistic. The function of courage is to resist fear so that love is not deflected from its task. Love and courage, then, are necessary so that life is sustained and fear subdued. If sentimental kindness could have its way, it would abolish both love and courage: love, since it is willing to accept life with all the shocks that the flesh is heir to, and courage, becuase it secures the work of love. At the same time, a realistic attitude toward life does not negate ideals, though in its willingness to tolerate the imperfect realization of ideals it differs from idealism.

When Chesterton remarked that this fully positive disposition toward Eskimoes was accounted for by his never having met any, he was alluding to the readiness with which we idealize what we do not see. The future is something we do not see; accordingly, we should be wary of our readiness to idealize it. The future is not yet, but derives its substance from the present. Therefore, we move confidently and realistically forward into the future only by being faithful to our stewardship of the present. Garrett Hardin's assertion that we are "trustees of the future" but we "can always produce more babies" illustrates a profound anxiety about the present and a use of the idea of the future as a magical haven of redemption for our sins against the living.

A metaphysics of realistic insight followed by love and courage would obviously commend itself more than one based on an inverted image of things seen in a mood of fear. But it is in the nature of fear to embrace the illusion that nonbeing has more dominance and force than being itself, in which case negative reactions seem more appropriate than positive ones. In other words, abortionists do not see their inverted metaphysics as inverted; they see it as the way they believe they should see it. Although reality is common to all there are nonetheless contradictory perceptions of it. Clearly an appeal to metaphysics alone is not enough to resolve the abortion debate. What are essential are love and courage, and yet love and courage must be anchored in a metaphysical intuition of being as it is.

A realistic resolution of the abortion struggle will come, and it will come, if not through insight, through outrage. Noonan contends that the aggressiveness of the abortionists "leads them to outrages, and these outrages supply us with fresh reasons for our cause and new recruits for our movement."[18] Man cannot remain ruled by his fears and subservient to nonbeing indefinitely. The positive core of his being, that inner region of his soul named "immortal diamond,"[19] will not allow it. In the end, he will say no to the continuing carnage. At that same moment will be born his yes to life.

NOTES

[1]John T. Noonan Jr., "The Dynamics of Anti-Abortionism," reprinted in part in *Life Letter* ed. J.P McFadden, No. 18, 15 December, 1977.

[2]Eleanor Pelrine, *Abortion in Canada* (Toronto: New Press, 1972), p. 113. Mrs. Pelrine took the quotation from Trudeau's *Approaches to Politics*.

[3]James Gustafson, "Interdependence and Human Limitations: Reflections by a Theologian on the 'Energy Crisis'," *Halifax Conference* - 1974.

[4]John Fordon, age 15, "Leaves are More Important," *Newsday*, 27 April 1970.

[5]Richard Neuhaus, *In Defense of People* (New York: Macmillan, 1971), p. 186.

[6]Newhaus, p. 187.

[7]Willard Gaylin and Mark Lappe, "Fetal Politics: The dabate on experimen-

ting with the unborn," *Atlantic* (May 1975), p.70.

[8]Gaylin, p. 66.

[9]Margaret Mead, "The Many Rights to Life," *Redbook* (July 1978), p. 109.

[10]Mead, p. 173.

[11]The story was carried by the Canadian Press in December of 1978.

[12]Paul Tillich, *The Courage to Be* (New Haven: Yale University Press, 1965), p. 66.

[13]William Barrett, *Irrational Man* (Garden City:Doubleday, 1962), p. 62.

[14]Martin Heidegger, *Introduction to Metaphysics* (Garden City: Doubleday, 1961), p. 111.

[15]Tillich, p. 78.

[16]Robert and Suzanne Massie, *Journey* (New York: Knopf, 1956).

[17]C.S. Lewis, *The Problem of Pain* (New York: Macmillan, 1976), p. 40.

[18]Noonan.

[19]Gerard Manley Hopkins: "This Jack, joke, poor potsherd, patch, matchwood, immortal, Is Immortal diamond.", from "That Nature is a Heraclitean Fire and the Comfort of the Resurrection," *Gerard Manley Hopkins* (London: Penguin, 1933), p. 66.

9.
Sex and the Repudiation of Incompleteness

Equal in dignity, complementary in mission.
—Pope John XXIII

The fact that in all cultures throughout history the person is identified as either a man or as a woman illustrates the fundamental importance society attaches to distinguishing the sexes. At the same time, nature covertly distinguishes the sexes in the chromosomes of each body cell of every individual. Sex reveals itself in perspective, being microscopic as well as macroscopic, atomic as well as anatomic, genetic as well as generic, personal as well as political. It is *dipolar* both in typology and in the manner in which it discloses that typology.

Sex embodies the power of procreation, with man and woman representing the two complementary types of the human species whose union reproduces the species. Yet sex means more than procreation, for it is a rich and vital source of human creativity. In addition, sex means dividedness, bi-sectedness, the insufficiency of the individual, the natural need of a helpmate; while at the same time, through its consanguineous ties with ancestry and future progeny, it transcends the plane of incompleteness and impermanence, and participates in aspects of the eternal and the infinite. Moreover, the sexes are at once similar and different, individualized and complementary, personal and supra-personal. Sex is, therefore, *paradoxical.*

Sex is also *cosmic.* Through sex man is intimately linked with the universal life of the cosmos. The ancient Chinese regarded sexual intercourse as the human counterpart of the cosmic process. The Greeks spoke of the universal principles of *Logos* and *Eros*, the Romans of *animus* and *anima*, the Oriental of *Yang* and *Yin*. Gender is employed in language to denote the sexual character of individual cosmic entities. The Oedipus and Elektra myths are based on the cosmic struggle between the Masculine and Feminine understood as eternal, dialectical principles.

Sex is *mystical* as well. The Bible describes the Church as the Bride of Christ, who is her Bridegroom. Fidelity to one's spouse symbolizes Christ's fidelity to His Church. In the various contexts of the sexual mysticism of the Near East and of India, the woman is mystically interpreted as an occasion for her lover to experience depths beyond depths of transcendent illumination, much in the way Dante saw Beatrice as a manifestation of some divine principle.

In sum, sex distinguishes man and woman, but it also implies something that is at once private and public, temporal and timeless, carnal and cosmic, manifest and mystical. It is a concept that is extraordinarily rich in both direct and analogical meaning, but in all its diverse implications always signifies differentiation and either present or prospective unification.

Therefore, it is indeed remarkable that a lavish amount of energy is expended in today's society in the interest of denying sexual differences and trivializing sex to the level where it is made to appear as little or nothing more than a political reality. Politics, needless to say, is a dangerous way of viewing the sexes because it gives power and partisanship too much prominence and obscures the fundamental importance of nature and man's historical experience. There are real differences between the sexes—a fact that empirical science amply corroborates—and these differences are important because they offer people indispensable opportunities for overcoming their incompleteness and isolatedness through a personal union, physical or spiritual, with their complementary other—a union that opens to even fuller, more transcendent unions. The current denial of sex differences, unfortunately, not only deprives individuals of opportunities for such personally fulfilling union, but can only further deepen their already deep sense of incompleteness and alienation.

Ours is an era of power. Perhaps the most compelling documentation of this point is in Lewis Mumford's *Pentagon of Power*, the culmination of a series of studies that began in 1934 with his *Technics and Civilization*. In this compendious and historic work, Mumford develops the five parts of the pentagon that characterizes the present era: Political absolutism, Power (energy), Productivity, pecuniary Profit, and Publicity. If his diagnosis is correct—and there can be little doubt that it is correct to an important extent—then the political, ideological, and commercial interests that dominate contemporary civilization provide a context within which the widespread identification of sex with power is virtually unavoidable.

Mumford describes a "happening" staged at an American university, which although of small importance in itself, exquisitely symbolizes the modern penchant to de-nature sex and enshrine a power surrogate in its place. In this "happening" a group of women build a nest while a group of men erect a tower. Then each destroys the other's work. The players climax their performance by surrounding an automobile covered with strawberry jam and licking it off. The evident symbolic meaning: the obliteration of traditional sex roles and the erotic celebration of a new courtship—with power (How sweet it is!).

Symbolism aside, consider Susan Brownmiller's *Against Our Will: Men, Women, and Rape*, a book that was serialized in four national magazines and won its authoress innumerable accolades including her selection to *Time* magazine's twelve Women of the Year for 1975. In it, Miss Brownmiller argues that all forms of oppression have their origin in unequal physical power, which continues to define and distort the relationships between the sexes; that marriage is rooted in the fear of rape; and that rape "is nothing more or less than a conscious process of intimidation by which *all men* keep *all women* in a state of fear."[2] She equates the male's physical difference with power, and that power with oppression and rape. Her solution to the dilemma, however, is not that men use their energies in more positive ways to improve their relationship with women, but that women work to gain a counterbalancing political power as a way of "fighting back". She envisions female political power as the appropriate instrument for neutralizing male physical power. By using one form of power to offset another, she believes the differences between the sexes can be effectively eradicated. The alleged unremitting violent proclivities of *all* men notwithstanding,

Miss Brownmiller, confident in the power of politics, concludes that the proper relation of the sexes is achievable—and it is one which is the same in all times, places, and circumstances: namely, of perfect equality and mutual independence. Her excessive preoccupation with power prevents her from imagining any real, integrative solution to the problems between the sexes.

Sociologist Ann Oakley arrives at the same identitarian ideal, though from an opposite premise. "Biology," she contends, "demonstrates the identity of male and female." "Neither the phallus nor the womb are organs of one sex only: the female phallus (the clitoris) is the biological equivalent of the male organ, and men possess a vestgial womb."[3] Using the same "logic", one could argue that since human embryos have pharyngeal gill slits, they and fish are one and the same. Miss Oakley does not distinguish between *identity* and *similarity*. Neither does she discuss normality of functioning. The same lack of scientific precision is found in Dr. David Reuben's popular book *Any Woman Can*. Reuben declares the "Every embryo starts out as female." His point is that since the male embryo lacks a developed penis it is similar and therefore identical to the female. The fact of the matter, however, is that sex coding is inscribed in the chromosomes, not the sex organs, and takes place at conception rather than long after implantation. Moreover, the idea that one sex can be defined by its not having a penis is a particular Freudian view that has been universally discredited.

Such unscientific assertions of scientists and independent researchers that the sexes are or ought to be identical are often accepted as constituting the last word on the subject. Ian Robertson asserts in his text book on sociology, for example, that the idea of inherent sexual difference is, in informed circles, virtually obsolete: "The present consensus among psychologists is that there may be some *predispositions* toward minor differences in the behavior of the sexes at birth but that these differences can easily be overriden by cultural learning."[4] In support of this statement he refers to Maccoby and Jacklin[5] who, as a matter of record, actually go to great length to show the important modes of behavior of the sexes, such as male aggression, *do* have a biological component. Not even Miss Brownmiller, hopeful as she is of "denying rape a future", believes that rape can "easily be overriden by cultural learning". And what woman of normal human sensibility could possibly regard the male's propensity to commit this violent act as a "minor difference?"

A similar kind of text-book editorializing once prompted C.S. Lewis to write his diatribe on society's conditioners, which he titled *The Abolition of Man*. A contemporary disciple of Lewis could take Robertson's citation and work up *The Abolition of Sex*. And who would be included in this alleged "consensus" of psychologists? No one, it would appear, of any scientific distinction. Take medical psychologist John Money, for instance, who is often touted as the leading proponent of the view that sex differences are culturally determined. Money maintains that the male hormone androgen not only shapes the external genitals but also "programs" parts of the brain, so that some types of behavior may come more naturally to one sex than the other. Moreover, Money is not timid when he speaks of biological differences between the sexes; he calls menstruation, gestation, lactation, and impregnation "imperative differences".[6]

The current scientific data offer no escape from the conclusion that sexual differences in aggression are strongly related to irreversible differences in the central nervous systems of men and women that are generated before birth.[7] The objective evidence points consistently to the relationship between the male hormone androgen and increased aggression, on the one hand, and the female hormone and reduced aggression, on the other.[8]

Psychological Abstracts lists some 15,000 studies a year on the subject of "Human Sex Differences". Each week new knowledge is gained on the differences between the sexes and new suggestions are offered as to how this knowledge can benefit both individuals and society. At the same time, however, and on a level decisively less scholarly, the case for sexual sameness is proposed, packaged and promulgated through the media and through the works of ideologically oriented individuals. Sociologist Steven Goldberg, for example, calls attention to this fact when he asserts that no serious woman biologist or anthropologist has offered her support for the theroies of such feminist writers as Millett, Greer, Firestone, Figes, Janeway, Mitchell, and to a lesser extent, De Beauvoir.

The striking contrast of these two radically dissimilar approaches exemplifies an unbridgeable duality that exists in our culture, one of unmixable philosophies, separating the serious scholar from the popular ideologue and, quite often, dividing an individual's own common sense convictions from his desire to have the fashionable outlook. Susan Brownmiller herself exemplifies the latter dualism when, in the very same book, she contradicts her *theoretical* indictment of all men by her *personal* acknowledgement of all the men—including the man with whom she was living—who sympathetically and generously supported her in writing the book. Psychologist Rhoda Lorand cites an example of how the same dualism affects New York educators who privately express consternation about a mandatory co-educational gym, yet dare not openly oppose it. She also refers to how the same phenomenon alienates school children from their teachers (and from their own moral sensibilities): In a TV program, nine-year old boys and girls express to an interviewer their dislike of co-educational gym classes and their preference for the segregated gym classes. The school principal then intervenes and explains to the children that they must learn to like the new arrangement because there are no longer boys and girls or men and women but only children and adults.

Science, understanding and insight are one thing; power, politics, and propaganda quite another. Yet, on the subject of sex, the two are so finely interwoven in the present culture that it is often very difficult for people to tell them apart. As a result, it is not uncommon for people to entertain attitudes about the sexes that are incompatible hybrids of insight and ideology, fact and fantasy, history and hysteria.

In an age that is characterized by its penchant for and praise of power, it is inevitable that people would seek to re-make or re-model sex through modes that are themselves expressions of power—technology and political legislation.[10] Yet the question of nature, similarities, and differences of the sexes is essentially an objective one, drawing from anthropology, biology, physiology, psychology, and various other arts and sciences that evolve independently of those current concerns Lewis Mumford symbolizes by his metaphor, "pentagon of power". The serious-minded people who discuss sex do not begin with the supposition that there cannot or should not be differences between the sexes and then distort their data to suit that supposition. They are reality-oriented in their thinking and the difficulties that evolve in their discussion can be settled, at least theoretically, by improving and refining their understanding of the objective data. Difficulties and problems do indeed arise, but where the object of study is a common human experience of the sexes, dialogue is potentially very fruitful.

When research psychologists Eleanor Maccoby and Carol Jacklin, in their classic study, *The Psychology of Sex Differences*, conclude that the male's greater aggression has a biological component, they support their thesis on three objective and verifiable levels: 1) that this difference manifests ifself in similar ways in man and subhuman primates; 2) that it is cross-culturally universal; and 3) that levels of aggression are responsive to hormones.[11] They are also concerned about whether adults reinforce or "shape" aggression in boys more than in girls. However, they find no evidence for this and suggest that the contrary may be true. The available evidence they study indicates that adults do not accept or approve aggression in either sex; they either react equally against aggression in both sexes or they react more strongly against boys' aggression on the grounds that boys are naturally more strong and prone to fight, and therefore must be kept under closer control. Although strong negative reactions by parents and teachers may actually serve to reinforce aggression in some boys,[12] this is not what is generally meant when it is alleged that adults "shape" the aggressive behavior of the two sexes differently. What is usually meant is that adults encourage aggressive behavior more in boys, and this is not supported by the evidence. Maccoby and Jacklin conclude, therefore, that the negative evidence on differential socialization on this point "has strengthened the case for biological origins of the sex differences in aggression."

Maccoby and Jacklin also find evidence that there is a genetic basis for the fact that girls have greater verbal ability than boys and that boys excel both in visual-spatial ability and in mathematics. Recent research on the structure and functioning of the brain has provided an interesting corroboraton of this view. The two hemispheres of the brain appear to develop differently in males and females. For most male brains (for right-handed people) the areas that control spatial functions are concentrated mainly on the right side of the brain while the areas that control language are concentrated largely on the left. In girls, control for these two functions appears to be distributed equally between right and left hemispheres. Thus, the lateralization of spatial and linguistic functions appears to be different in the sexes, being specialized and relatively concentrated in one or another cerebral hemisphere in the male, and less and more uniformly distributed in the female.

Marian McGlone, a psychologist at Ontario's Western University, studies men and women who suffered unilateral brain lesions. She found that after left-hemisphere damage, right-handed males were significantly more impaired than right-handed females in elementary language production and comprehension, in verbal intelligence and verbal memory. She also found that after right-hemisphere lesions, non-verbal intelligence was impaired in men but not in women. According to Dr. McGlone, the data suggests that there is greater hemisphere specialization for both verbal and non-verbal functions in the adult male than in the adult female.[13]

Because of the differences in the lateralization of functions in the two halves of the brain, the verbal and spatial functions are more likely to come into conflict with each other in women, and more likely to be separated from each other in men. Dr. Sandra Witelson of McMaster University advocates different methods of teaching reading to boys and girls, suggesting that a teaching approach that combines phonetics with the "look-say" approach might help to better integrate verbal and spatial skills.

To illustrate man's innate inclination to excel in spatial skills, let us consider chess, a game which demands a great capacity for imagining and recalling highly complicated spatial movements. When the United States Chess Federation published its recent list of Chess Masters and top players, no women were listed among the 191 names—and none ever have been. Yet, not only have women actively competed in chess for many decades (the first American Women's Chess conference was held in New York City in 1906), but they have received strong encouragement to do so by various chess promoting organizations as well as by governments, especially the Soviet Union. Nonetheless, female play is so inferior to top level male performance that the World Chess Federation offers special women's competition at a much lower standard than for men.

Women, on the other hand, seem much more at home in the realm of the concrete, that is, the tangible order of reality, especially in dealing with other people. They are more creative in life than in speculative fields, in dealing with facts than with ideas, in the spoken word than the abstract hypothesis. Amaury de Riencourt writes:

> Women tend more toward conformity than men—which is why they often excel in such disciplines as spelling and punctuation where there is only one correct answer, determined by social authority. Higher intellectual activities, however, require a mental independence and power of abstraction that they usually lack, not to mention a certain form of aggressive boldness of the imagination which can only exist in a sex that is aggressive for biological reasons . . . [14]

Women, as Steven Goldberg states, are the "directors of societies' emotional resources."[15] They are more naturally integrated, less one-sided than men. And this difference is consistent with the differences in brain structure and functioning in men and women that is currently under study.[16]

Objective evidence concerning the differences between the sexes offers people light in their never ending quest to become more aware of what it means to be a sexual being. To eschew this evidence—in the name of a mere equality of attribution or for whatever ideological cause—is to take flight from one's own nature and consequently embark on a course that has no real objective. Against such a self-destructive course Midge Decter has responded with this impassioned jeremiad: "There is no more radical nor desperately nihilistic statement to issue forth from the lips of humans than that there are no necessary differences between the sexes."[17]

The philosophical, psychological, physiological, sociological, and creative differences between the sexes have been extensively studied, researched, and documented, and are striking and undeniable.[18] What is more, the recognition and proper utilization of these differences is necessary for the harmonious and creative functioning of society. George Gilder asserts that "differences between the sexes are the single most important fact of human society." Margaret Mead states: "If any human society—large or small, simple or complex, based on the most rudimentary hunting and fishing, or on the whole elaborate interchange of manufactured products—is to survive, it must have a pattern of social life that comes to terms with the differences between the sexes." Steven Goldberg adds: "Sex is the single most decisive determinant of personal identity; it is the first thing we notice about another person and the last thing we forget."[19]

The question, then: "Why the denial of a fact so fundamental to the civilized life of society?'' As we have noted, we live in an age that exalts power and freedom. Consequently, ideas such as ''biology'', ''nature'', ''destiny'', ''type'', and so forth, all seem unduly limiting and contradict the temper of the times. People want to have the power to free themselves from artificial categories and cramping stereotypes; indeed, from limitations of any kind. Nonetheless, if human history has left us any wisdom it is that we cannot transcend our fate until we first accept it.

In addition, modern technology has lightened or freed us from many of our burdens. But at the same time, it has robbed many of the conviction that menial work has a human and even sacred value. As a result, it has become fashionable in some circles to label domestic housework as demeaning and raising a family as stifling and personally unfulfilling. In such circles, then, where the technological displacement of nature is particularly evident, the nature of sexual differences seems less and less important.

There is a more personal or existential reason that helps to explain why sex differences are unwelcome. The woman who has been treated unfairly by men or by male laws, let us say, may come to view the idea that men are naturally and immutably different as an inexcusable pretext for their unjust behavior. She may then, out of an understandable enthusiasm for justice, argue that there are no immutable differences between men and women, and that all sex differences are merely the result of the way male dominated cultures have socialized people. She may agree with Kate Millett who says, ''It is time that we realized that the whole structure of male and female personality is entirely imposed by social conditioning'' (this remark, unfortunately, is self-contradictory since there can be no personal *realization* where the *entire* personality is *socially conditioned*: not having a mind of one's own precludes the possibility of self-awareness). But her agreeement with Ms. Millett may be best explained psychologically by the fact that an ideology that denies real sex differences is attractive to her only because it happens to offer an immediate answer to her emotional needs. Such a view often places too much hope in the power of politics and too little in the power of the woman herself to deal with her problem, which may really be more personal than political.

In a deeper sense, however, difference does not necessarily mean advantage. Difference, in itself, is ambiguous. In the practical encounters people have with one another it could mean an opportunity to assume one's advantage or it could mean an opportunity for giving. A man who has more money than another might try to exploit him or, then, again, he might give some of his money to him. The difference itself is morally neutral. By the same token, a man might be stronger phsycially than a woman. He may harm her, or again, he might protect her from harm.

A purely political interpretation of the differences between the sexes is ill-advised for three reasons: First, because it impugns everything history, science, and art have taught us about the sexes and obliges us to inaugurate a new society based on nothing more than a gratuitous hypothesis; second, because it fails to recognize the positive powers peculiar to each sex and surrenders to politics powers that really belong to the person; third, because it is regressive in that it pessimistically assumes that difference will always mean advantage, something that is true only in the inter-species struggles of the sub-human world.

"The first and simplest of the paradoxes," writes Chesterton, is the fact that "two things being different implies that they are similar."[20] We say that the hare and the tortoise differ in the quality of their swiftness only because we know they are both in motion. We do not say that a hare is faster than an isosceles triangle; they have nothing in common. Likewise, the fact that men and women differ in any number of ways does not negate similarity, it implies it.

A good marital realtionship requires a blend of love and authority. Although love presupposes sameness, authority presupposes difference. Yet, they do not exclude one another; in fact they work to protect each other; love protects authority from degenerating into authoritarianism, authority protects love from sinking into an impractical idealism.

Authority is never complete in itself; in order to remain fully human it must remain open to sympathy, love, and concern for others. Through Mary's expressed solicitude at Cana, Christ agreed to authorize His first public miracle for the concrete benefit of the wedding guests. It can be misleading to evaluate authority and love unequally. In order for them to maintain their personal functioning, they must complement each other. The important concern, therefore, with regard to the sexes, is that male authority not be intransigent and that female love not be impractical. In conceiving authority as an exclusive province of one sex and love as the peculiar province of the other, one precludes the possibility of authority and love operating in a complementary way that allows the sexes to work together.

Another paradox that belongs to sex involves the active-passive polarity. Whenever one partner initiates, the initiation is frustrated if the other is unwilling to receive. In sexual intercourse the male is the more active agent, analogous to the more active role of the spermatazoon in penetrating and fertilizing the more passive (though not exclusively passive) ovum. Yet if we consider the moment of childbirth, the roles are reversed, the woman actively exerting herself in delivering the child, whereas the man (who assists in the delivery) passively receives the child into his arms. Men and women should be relatively active or passive in accord with those activities which are their proper dominion.

When a woman attracts a man, she exemplifies an active quality that has its natural effect in the passive receptiveness of the man. Yet the man may, as a result of his passive acceptance of the woman's attractiveness, activate himself toward the woman who is now passively disposed to accept his advances. The active-passive polarity is an alternating dialogue. It is not the case that either man or woman is simply active or passive; they are active or passive in different ways and at different times.

Finally, there is the paradox that brings together the mind and the heart: the mind which impersonally classifies and categorizes, and the heart that understands in a more personal manner. There is much talk these days about the dangers of categorizing and stereotyping the sexes.[21] Yet the real danger is not in the abstract appraisal of the sexes itself, but in believing that this kind of appraisal apprehends their whole, existential truth. We must allow the heart to know the person. But the mind has a role to play as well. It is false to think that the mind cannot apply itself to the subject of sex, that it cannot grasp—though imperfectly—the intelligibility of sex. Many people insist that they prefer to be known as human rather than as male or female, since, they feel, "male" and "female" are but empty, intellectual stereotypes. Yet, is one not stereotyped if he is labelled a human? Jean-Paul Sartre found the idea of "human" far too stereotypic for his own philosophy and replaced it with what he believed to be a broader expression—*être-pour-soi* (being-for-itself). Ironically, his *être-pour-soi* is too narrowly stereotypic for the Christian who also sees man as a "being-for-others". Similarly, many feminists who strenuously oppose "stereotyping" belong to groups which are themselves so arbitrarily stereotyped (abortion on demand, lesbianism, etc.) that they offend and alienate other women. It was this kind of ideological self-stereotyping, by the way, that caused the celebrated split of the International Woman's Conference in Houston in 1978. We begin to approach the elusive truth of men and women only when we learn how to integrate the mind with the heart.

The richness of the notion of sex and the kinds of humanizing spiritual or physical relationships that are possible between the sexes, is something that can be appreciated—and then but partially—only in an intuition. Empirical science is analytic, and while it is possible to pass from synthesis to analysis, it is quite another thing to attempt the passage from analysis to synthesis. Scientific analysis can corroborate some of what man has experienced through intuition about sex, but it cannot refute it. The fullness of sex is akin to a symphony which a composer or a conductor can envision in a single intuitive flash in its balance and detail, its analogical evocations, and its paradoxical intricacies.

Because their complementarity offers an indispensable opportunity for achieving a great realization of personal wholeness, men and women naturally assume certain obligations to each other which we may express in the form of a general principle, namely, that whatever inclinations and activities may be their proper dominion, men and women should exercise them in a way that is always open to their complementary opposites. Neither male authority nor female empathy, male aggressiveness nor female receptiveness, male prowess nor female endurance, male genius in the arts and sciences nor female genius in life are sufficient unto themselves. Each one, in the interest of being more fully human, must be wed to its respective opposite, so that two incomplete, one-sided parts may form a richer, more rewarding, and more realistic whole. The rightful destiny of men and women, in the words of Pope John XXIII, is to be "equal in dignity, complementary in mission." Russian existentialist Nicolas Berdyaev expresses much the same philosophy when he writes:

> The masculine element is essentially creative and the feminine birth-giving. But neither in generation nor in creativeness can the masculine and the feminine principles be isolated; they intereact and complete

one another. Both through creation and procreation man strives to attain the androgynous wholeness of his being, though he can never reach it on the earthly plane.[22]

Equality "in dignity" and "in humanity" is not in the least threatened by the recognition of real differences between the sexes. However, if equality is taken in an exclusively political sense, the fear may arise that difference and equality are indeed incompatible, for broadly stated political legislation (the proposed Equal Rights Amendment comes to mind) cannot begin to do justice to the various shadings of paradoxical, companionate, and complementary differences that distinguish the sexes. In fact, the ERA movement has been thus far halted, according to its opponents, precisely because it threatens to deprive women of rights that they have already achieved.

It is difficult to talk or write about any reality and even begin to do justice to it. In the case of sex, the frustration is felt all the more acutely. The essential quality of the real is that it is always richer and more elusive than what we can ever grasp. There is "man" and there is "woman;" God is always masculine, and women belong to the "distaff". But just when we think we have spotted an intolerably one-sided approach to sex, we remember that there is the "bride and the bridegroom" and that the man who accompanies the beautiful woman is *her* escort. Sex is never simple; it is always paradoxical. And if "*man*handle" means to handle recklessly, then we must not forget that "to husband" means to embrace with care—a husband husbands his wife. The apparent inconsistencies of language reflect the pardoxical richness of sex. We name things by some aspect of their outward appearance though our words never do justice to their interior depth and diversity (we use the term "day" to include both "day" and "night", just as we use the generic term "man" to include both "men" and "women").

The difference between paradox and contradiction is not always evident. A paradox is an apparent contradiction that really contains a prodigality of meaning. A contradiction is a logical indication of a real impossibility. The fact that a good relationship between a man and a woman requires the harmonious integration of authority and love, initiation and reception, mind and heart, illustrates this paradoxical nature of sex; the notion that a person can combine only one of any of these pairs with happiness or fulfillment is a contradiction.

Susan Brownmiller states that the proper relationship between the sexes is perfect equality although all men are predators and all women their victims. Valerie Solanis argues that men are absolutely inferior to women except that men have a genius for public relations which they use to seduce women into thinking that men are women and women are men.[23] Gloria Steinem and Bella Abzug lobby for equal rights on the basis that biology is not destiny and oppose the draft for women on the grounds that waging war is a peculiarly male mode of behavior.[24] Are these argumentations paradoxical or contradictory? And how should we evaluate the popular dictum that women were doormats for 10,000 years until they were "liberated" by the Pill? Or Chesterton's *bon mot*: "Twenty million young women rose to their feet with the cry, 'We will not be dictated to,' and promptly became stenographers.'"?

On the other side, we hear the deathless words of Professor Henry Higgins: "Why can't a woman be more like a man?" Freud states that women "refuse to accept the fact that they are castrated." Rousseau argues that "The whole education of women ought to be relative to men." A prominent psychiatrist writes that "A woman is a uterus surrounded by a supporting organism and directing personality."[25] Are these remarks not barbarously one-sided, reflecting an attitude that contradicts the true paradoxical nature of sex and the proper dialogical relationship between the sexes?

A lived contradiction leads to anxiety. An obsession with one side of sex is always accompanied by a repression of the other side. A person who lives this obsession-repression syndrome must inevitably experience emotional contradictions and deep anxieties, for one cannot deny one important aspect of reality and still retain an outlook toward life that is healthy and realistic. People try to anesthetize themselves to certain differences between the sexes because these differences remind them of their own insufficiency, limitedness, and dependence, on the one hand, and on the other, their need to embark on the difficult and painful task of balancing and reconciling opposites, not only in their own relationships with people of the opposite sex but within themselves as well. Growth and integration are always painful, whereas anesthesia is ever tempting.

Paradox, however, invites us to enjoy new levels of freedom, and larger and deeper unifications with the "other". We speak of "man and woman", "husband and wife", "mother and child", "father and son", "God and creation", "Christ and His Church", and so on. What is essential to all these couplings is the "and", this unseen, mysterious factor across which love is transmitted and through which unity is achieved.

The sexual "and" implies that men and women need each other for their fulfillment (spiritually, that is, and not necessarily physically). Acceptance of this "and" is the acceptance of one's own limitatons as well as the limitations of the other. Hence the paradox: Completion begins only through the mutual acceptance of incompletion.

In its analogical sense, sex is the polar expression of a fundamental principle that pervades all levels of being from the positive and negative fusions of atoms to the relationship between man, the family, the community, or the church with God. Even the Trinity itself exemplifies this polarity. Karl Stern reminds us that "Nature is the soil of Grace, and the love of the sexes is a prototype of divine Love."[27] It is not surprising, then, that substantial confirmation is found concerning the complementary differences of the sexes in all fields from art to zoology.

To see the complementary differences between the sexes represents a vision that leads to ever larger visions. The need for union does not end with sex; rather, sex prefigures unions that are more mystical and ever more profound. Our culture conveys the illusions that we can gain freedom through power and that the individual alone can achieve self-sufficiency. Sex, which literally means bi-sected,[28] offers a way of love and integration that begins in the humble acknowledgement of our limitations and incompleteness. Through differences we escape the prison of our own solitude and begin to discover, to our eternal delight, that our opposites do not constitute our opposition but offer us continuing opportunities for growth and personal fulfillment; for our minds and hearts are far more capacious than we could ever have surmised.

NOTES

[1]Lewis Mumford, *The Pentagon of Power* (New York: Harcourt, Brace, Jovanovich, 1970), p. 365.

[2]Susan Brownmiller, *Against Our Will: Men, Women, and Rape* (New York: Simon & Schuster, 1975), p. 15.

[3]Ann Oakley, *Sex, Gender, and Society* (San Francisco: Harper & Row,

1972), p 18.

[4]Ian Robertson, *Sociology* (New York: World Publishers, 1977), p. 292.

[5]E.E. Maccoby and C.H. Jacklin, *The Psychology of Sex Differences* (Stanford: Stanford University Press, 1974).

[6]John Money, *Man & Woman, Boy & Girl* (Baltimore: John Hopkins, 1972).

[7]For a discussion on "The Hormonal Factor" and references to current research on this point see: Steven Goldberg, *The Inevitablity of Patriarchy* (New York: William Morrow, 1973-4), pp. 74-99.

[8]See: Murray S. Work and Hilliard Rogers, "Effect of Estrogen Level on Food-Seeking Dominance Among Male Rats," *Journal of Comparative and Physiological Psychology*, 79:3 (1972).

[9]Dr. Rhoda L. Lorand, in a statement to the Minnesota Committee for Positive Education, p. 6.

[10]This is not to indict in any way either technology or political legislation. They are both needed and necessary. The point here is that neither technology or political legislation—indispensable as they are to current society—are instruments through which sex and the differences between the sexes can be understood. Sex is not an essentially technological or political reality. In various ways, however, writers such as Firestone, Guettel, Chessler, Millett, Francoeur suggest the contrary.

[11]Maccoby, 1974.

[12]See: Goldberg, p. 213: "I think that it would be more sensible for the feminist to argue that our society overrates manifestations of male genius and underrates manifestations of female genius rather than to argue that there are no differences in males and females engendering the two . . ."

[13]Marian Jeannette McGlone, "Sex differences in functional brain symmetry after damage to the left and right hemispheres, " *Dissertation Abstracts International*, 1978 (Mar.), vol. 38 (6-B), 4471. See also McGlone, "Sex differences in functional brain symmetry," *Cortex*, 1978 (Mar.), Vol. 14 (1), 122-8.

[14]Amaury de Riencourt, *Sex and Power in History* (New York: McKay, 1974).

[15]Goldberg, pp. 228-9.

[16]Dr. Jerry Levy, a brain researcher of the University of Chicago's Department of Behavioral Sciences supports the Canadian studies on the difference in the lateralization of brain function in the sexes. See: *Quest/80*, "Men, Women, and the Brain," Vol. 4, No. 8, 1980 (Oct.), p. 93: ". . . males are in general superior at seeing invariance independent of context: concepts. They are good at maps and mazes and math: at rotating objects in their minds and perceiving three-dimensional objects in two-dimensional representations. They seem to be less dependent on situational variables for the solution of a problem: more narrowly focused, less distractible. Females, by contrast, are sensitive to context, good at picking up information that is incidental to a task that's set them, and distractible, which is *also* to say unblinkered by the demands of a particular goal. The are superior in certain important verbal skills—fluency, grammar, reading, for example. They have a better fine motor coordination. They are at an advan-

tage in reading the emotional content of faces. They are sensitive to odors and are extremely sensitive to the presence and variation of sound." For a scientifically detailed treatment and corroboration of sexual dimorphism see "Sexual Dimorphism," *Science*, Frederick Naftolin and Eleanore Butz eds. Vol. 211, No. 4488, 1981 (March 20).

[17]Midge Decter, *The New Chastity & Other Arguments against Women's Liberation* (New York: Berkley Medallion Books, 1972), pp. 212.

[18]For excellent and informative treatments on each of these areas see: Corinne Hutt, *Males and Females* (London: Penguin, 1972); Judith Bardwick, *Psychology of Women* (New York: Harper & Row, 1971); Paul Weiss *Sport: A Philosophic Inquiry* (Carbondale, Ill.: Southern Illinois University Press, 1969); George Gilder, *Sexual Suicide* (New York: Quadrangle, 1973); Karl Stern, *Flight From Woman* (New York: Farrar Straus, & Giroux, 1965); Margaret Mead, *Male and Female* (New York: William Morrow, 1958).

[19]Goldberg, p. 229.

[20]Hugh Kenner, *Paradox in Chesterton* (New York: Sheed & Ward, 1947), p. 25.

[21]A British Council of Churches prayer book which represses the traditional "Our *Father*" offers this prayer: "Make us aware of what we have done when we deny another's potential by categorizing that person in terms of sex."

[22]Nicolas Berdyaev, *The Destiny of Man*, tr. Natalie Duddington (New York: Harper & Row, 1960), p. 67.

[23] Valerie Solanis, "Excerpts from the SCUM Manifesto," *Sisterhood is Powerful*, Robin Morgan ed. (New York: Vintage, 1970), p. 515.

[24]See: Goldberg, p. 227: "There are feminists who try to have it both ways; they deny the importance of the biological basis of the behavior of the sexes, yet blame the world's war on the male characteristics of its leaders."

[25]Iago Galdston, 1958, in Mary Calderone ed. *Abortion in the United States*, p. 118.

[26]See: Rollo May *Love and Will* (New York: W.W. Norton, 1969), "But human beings cannot block off any important biological or emotional aspect of experience without developing an equivalent amount of inner anxiety." pp. 106-7

[27]Karl Stern, p. 224.

[28]According to W.W. Skeath in *Etymology of English Usage*, the probable original meaning of the word "sex" is "a division", from the Latin *secare*, to cut.

10.
Sexual Wholeness and the Denunciation of Self-Control

Of all sexual aberrations, chastity is the strangest.
—Anatole France

According to the fashionable wisdom which inscribes its moral epigrams on subway walls and other such places: "Chastity is its own punishment", "Chaste makes waste", and "Virtue can hurt you".[1] Indeed, so widespread is such an attitude that it is customary for many authors of books on sexual morality, among them even Catholic priests, to refrain from mentioning the very word chastity, let alone identify it as a rewarding virtue. "Chastity," as C.S. Lewis notes—and it is truer today than when he said it in 1952—"is the most unpopular of the Christian virtues."[2] And the reason for its ranking last and least in the lexicon of virtues in vogue is not difficult to understand. Chastity is unpopular because it is so difficult and so contrary to our instincts. The traditional rule of chastity demands that sexual expressions be restricted to one's marital partner. Thus, one's options are painfully limiting: Either marriage, with complete faithfulness to one's spouse, or else total abstinence.

Perhaps nowhere else in the domain of morality is there so broad a gap between rule and practice as there is with respect to chastity. Today, sexual pleasure outside of marriage is so common that many people—including Ann Landers and other influential moralists—simply believe that sex cannot be brought under human control. This unduly pessimistic view leads logically to the popular position, espoused by organizations such as Planned Parenthood, that sex can be controlled only technologically, that is, through contraception, sterilization, and abortion.

Given this technological approach to controlling the uses and the consequences of sex, virtue is thereby extroverted into something outside of man, a process that is unfortunately accompanied by no small degree of self-alienation. Aldous Huxley prophesied in his anti-utopian nightmare, *Brave New World*, that human virtues would be replaced by drugs: "Anybody can be virtuous now," he wrote. "You can carry at least half your morality about in a bottle. Christianity without tears—that's what *soma* is."[3] The current reality, however, may be even more frightening and self-alienating. Virtue, at least in sexual matters, is now even further removed from the individual, having been placed in the hands of professional technicians, though it appears reasonably close by, being only a telephone appointment away.

The willingness to replace human virtue with technological virtue is also consistent with a basic assumption of contemporary society, namely, that making life easier is synonymous with progress. Such an assumption, needless to say, stands in flat contradiction with willingly accepting the difficulties involved in developing the human virtue of chastity. Consequently, by assuming that progress means making life easier, society inevitably concludes that chastity is contrary to progress. As a result, society adopts unchastity as a moral norm, although a kind of moderate, socially responsible unchastity that asks nothing more of people than they not use sex to hurt one another. Dr. Mary Seeman of Toronto's Clarke Institute of Psychiatry advises that "healthy sexuality means arriving at some middle ground between the two extremes of promiscuity and celibacy".[4] Such advice is typical of the current attitude toward sex. A middle ground between promiscuity and celibacy is not a virtuous mean between two extremes. Rather, it is a statistical average that is symptomatic not of virtue, but of mediocrity.

One of the bitterest ironies of modern life is that by trying to make life easier—in the name of progress—society does not make life easier or better, only more mediocre. Novelist Walker Percy makes the following comment on this widespread desire on the part of society to make a virtue of low aim:

> Our civilization has achieved a distinction of sorts. It will be
> remembered not for its technology nor even its wars but for its novel
> ethos. Ours is the only civilization in history which has enshrined
> mediocrity as its national ideal. Others have been corrupt, but leave
> it to us to invent the most undistinguished of corruptions.

Chastity, then, is unpopular because it is difficult, contrary to our
instincts, and is counter to the prevailing ethos. But this is not to say
that chastity is not important or even crucial, indeed, even necessary.
Thomas Aquinas makes the point that "the more necessary something
is, the more the order of reason must be preserved in it."[6] The eminent
sensibleness of this observation is perhaps more evident today than it
was when it was offered in the Thirteenth Century. Air and water, for
example, are necessary for the continuation of life. It becomes all the
more important, therefore, that we do not pollute our air and water with
toxic chemicals and harmful radiation. In other words, it is of the ut-
most importance that whatever we do that affects our environment is
always done in accordance with reason. Nonetheless, because of financial and technological difficulties, our instinctual laziness, and the prevailing demands for production and consumption, we continue to pollute
our environment.

Sex is also necessary for the continuation of life; thus, the fundamental
importance of reason being preserved in it. Psychotherapist Rollo May
expresses the point this way: "Surely an act that carries as much power
as the sexual one, and power in the critical area of passing on one's name
and species, cannot be taken as banal and insignificant except by doing
violence to our natures, if not to 'nature' itself."[7] But sex also contains
ramifications that bear upon the physical, moral, and spiritual health of
the individual and society. That sex be in accord with reason, then, is
not only a matter of fundamental importance, but one of virtually comprehensive importance.

The essence of any virtue is that it be moderated by reason. Chastity
is simply the virtue that brings man's sexual appetite into accord with
reason. It is not the renunciation of sex, but simply the right use of it.
According to Aquinas, chastity chastizes the sexual appetite, which, like
a child, needs curbing.[8] Through such disciplining, chastity realizes the
order of reason. By defining chastity in relation to reason, we do not
intend to suggest that man ought to conduct his life rationalistically, ac-

cording to an abstract blueprint which is the product of purely rational thought. Such a life would not, properly speaking, be a moral life. "Reason" should be understood here not abstractly or idealistically, but realistically, that is to say, with reference to reality. Reason, in communion with reality, allows us to know what we must do and what we must avoid so that we may live in terms of who we really are. Josef Pieper, an expert in the Scholastic concept of virtue, remarks that by living in accordance with reason, man is able "to keep himself in himself."[9] Reason, therefore, allows a man to achieve and maintain self-possession, the opposite of the current self-alienation that results when man allows technological power to displace human virtue.

It is secular society, as a matter of fact, which insists that man live rationalistically. And it is precisely this rationalistic approach that furnishes man with no end of excuses not to discipline his sexual appetite, marry, be faithful, or have children. Secular man comes to regard virtue, marriage, fidelity—all of them—as severely limiting. He demands full and unfettered freedom. And yet he finds no satisfaction in the experience of such freedom.

T.S. Eliot has noted that secular man is so terrified of reality both outside and within that he seeks escape "by dreaming of systems so perfect that no one will need to be good."[10] Yet man needs to be good, just as profoundly as he needs to be himself. And in order to be good, he must accept reality. Therefore, he must employ reason not rationalistically as a way of avoiding reality, but realistically in an effort to understand his own human nature and the virtues he needs in order to live a truly good and moral life.

If the notion of "chastity" has become so unpopular that the very word "chastity" causes uneasiness or embarrassment, we may refer to another culture in which this phenomenon has not occurred. The Russian word for chastity—*tselomudrie*—means, by derivation, "the wisdom of wholeness". To the Russian mind, *tselomudrie* means maintaining the integrity of sex, while its opposite means dissipation, an extreme degree of the fractionalization of sex-energy, alienating it from man's integral nature. Russian philosopher Nicolas Berdyaev writes: "Only in so far as he [man] is complete is he chaste, wise and Sophian in his perfect wholeness. As a . . . divided being, he is not chaste, not wise, and is doomed to disharmony, to passionate longing and dissatisfaction.''[11]

Because man is, through and through, a sexual being, chastity has implications for the whole of the human personality. Chastity means the integrity of the sexual person. The chaste person who gives himself to his spouse does so wholly, without holding back anything for himself. He refuses to allow his sexual powers to be fractionalized, to be divided into pieces, giving part to the other but retaining another part for himself. Contraception is contrary to chastity because it divides partner from procreator and separates the giver from his own gift. Being whole, the chaste man experiences things in his wholeness. Things do not merely stimulate him; they resound in his whole being. Therefore, he experiences more than pleasure, which is associated with a part; he experiences joy. He experiences life more fully and joyfully because he experiences it with everything he is.

The virtue of chastity allows man to realize the order of reason in sexual matters. Unchastity, therefore, is a natural enemy of reason and all that reason involves: understanding, counsel, judgment, and command. And since reason works in tandem with the will, unchastity also impairs the operation of the will. Aquinas lists the ill effects of unchastity or lust as blindness of mind, rashness, thoughtlessness, inconstancy, inordinate self-love, hatred of God, excessive love of this world, and abhorrence or despair of a future world. He compares unchastity with the lion who, catching sight of the stag, cannot desire or think of anything but his anticipated meal. The lion does not enjoy the aesthetic beauty of the stag, nor is he concerned with the stag's desire to continue living.

At the core of unchastity is a selfishness or a self-interest that militates against an objective appraisal of things. Unchastity poisons the cognitive process and renders man less capable of perceiving reality selflessly and disinterestedly. For the unchaste person, as Josef Pieper explains, it is as if "the 'window' of the soul has lost its 'transparency', that is, its capacity for perceiving existence, as if a selfish interest had covered it, as it were, with a film of dust.''[12]

For those who have been frustrated in their attempts to discuss a reasonable basis for moral norms with defenders of abortion, it is important to keep in mind that a major root of the abortion movement is the unchastity that brought about the wave of unintended and unwanted pregnancies which created the demand for abortion. Since blindness of mind, rashness, and the rest are necessary companions of unchastity, it is no mystery why many abortionists are seemingly blind to the objective value of the human unborn and prefer to resolve the abortion issue not in terms of objective values, but in terms of private choice.

A British physician, writing in the medical newspaper *Pulse*, argues that we can resolve many of today's moral problems simply by allowing lust to have its way. His argument reflects a lack of realism and consequently a lack of reasonableness that is truly exceptional, even for today: "If every man and every woman had as much sex as they wanted there would be less fighting, cheating, twisting and other forms of evil in the world." A more sober compatriot of the doctor, C.S. Lewis, once remarked that, "Surrender to all our [sexual] desires obviously leads to impotence, disease, jealousies, lies, concealment, and everything that is the reverse of health, good humour, and frankness."[13] If cultural history has anything to teach us it is that no civilization can endure whose citizens refuse to practice some form of sexual restraint. We do not need to discover any additional evidence that Venus and Mars are not strangers, a point Pascal made immortal when he remarked that, "If the nose of Cleopatra had been a little shorter the whole face of the world would have been changed."[14]

Another troublesome effect of unchastity—particularly pervasive unchastity—is the cynical belief that chastity, even if it were desirable, is, for most people, not even possible. This view does not accord with the historical experience of man; but it also contradicts everything that empirical science tells us about moral man. And since empirical science, apart from its own inherent validity, has a great deal of influence and respectability in our time, we are well advised to become better acquainted with what is known about the scientific basis for the possibility of chastity.

Evolutionary biologists agree that the evolutionary step from animals to man could not have taken place without the concomitant development of highly organized brain structures to inhibit and sublimate the powerful animalistic impulses and instincts which man has in common with all animals. Many brain researchers correlate this inhibitory capacity with the specific structure of the human forebrain. The Viennese psychiatrist Constantin von Economo drew attention to the fact that in man there exist parts of the forebrain which have no counterpart in the brains of animals, and that these parts represent not only additional brain tissue but new functions.[15]

Brain researchers, studying the behavioral effects caused by brain injuries of victims of World Wars I and II, have found evidence on a neurophysiological level for the possibility of ethical behavior in human beings. After massive damage to the tissue of both sides of that portion of the forebrain called the orbital brain, the victim loses his capacity to act ethically, morally, and responsibly. However, if the parts of the forebrain just above the orbital brain are still intact, the intellectual capacities remain unimpaired allowing the victim to make right judgments about good and evil although he no longer has the capacity to act in accordance with these moral judgments. Where there is symmetrical massive damage to this region of the forebrain, man loses his capacity to act rationally.

Such research makes clear two points: 1) that certain portions of the brain are unique to man and correlate with his capacity to reason, his capacity to make moral judgments, and his capacity to act on those judgments; 2) that in order for a man to retain his undisturbed capacity for acting morally, the orbital brain must be intact.

Other research shows that in the process of evolution, the decisive factor for controlling sexual impulses has migrated from the deeper parts of the brain—particularly the hypothalamus—to the peculiarly human parts of the forebrain. Scientists generally agree that although sexual impulses in the human also rise in the hypothalamus, man retains the possibility of integrating these impulses with his moral insights by using the unique and peculiarly human capacities of his forebrain.[16] Neurophysiologist Paul Chaucard finds that the sexuality of lower animals is entirely dominated by instincts or impulses that arise in the hypothalamus. He refers to an experiment with butterflies in which a piece of cotton is saturated with the odor of a female butterfly's ovaries, and how the male butterflies impulsively attempt to copulate with the cotton rather than the females that are equally accessible to them. Chaucard argues that in man the brain is the chief sexual organ, being able to accept or reject sexual impulses that originate in the hypothalamus. He concludes, therefore, that sexual control humanizes sexuality by allowing reason to govern it. He writes in is book *Maîtrise sexuelle* (*Sexual Mastery*) that: "Animals have only to follow their instincts, man must devise what he will do; his instincts are little developed and he can in great measure discipline and master them.''[17]

It is paradoxical that contemporaneous with the discovery of the function of the frontal brain which allows man to inhibit his sexual impulses, is a growing public cry that sexual restraint is unnatural, unhealthy, inhuman. At the same time, man's capacity for self-control, especially in sexual matters, was well known to pagan philosophers in pre-scientific days. Plato, for example, spoke of man's tripartite soul which consists of *reason*, the 'forbidding principle' that reflects before it inhibits; *desire*, the unreflecting appetite which seeks its own gratification; and *spirit*, the propulsive faculty that transmits the verdict of reason to the appetite.[18]

Whereas it was clear to the ancients that man's appetites, especially sexual desire, could and should be governed by reason, certain modern thinkers, most notably Sigmund Freud, seem to champion the rights of appetite itself against the rule of reason. Critics of Freudian thinking contend that Freud tried to free man's pleasure principle, the *libido*, so that man could live uninhibited and unrepressed in his deep vital urges. As a corrective to this undue emphasis on the pleasure principle, another Viennese psychiatrist, Viktor Frankl, warns that the repression of the *spirit* of man may be more fatal and destructive of human personality than the repression of *libido*.[19] The *libido* can be so sublimated into the spirit, a notion perfectly consistent with recent scientific findings; the spirit, however, can only be suffocated by the *libido* let loose. Thus, Frankl makes a plea for the cultivation of not only depth-psychology but also, and indeed more urgently, of height-psychology. The pleasure principle is, he asserts, a psychological artifact, an ill-founded invention of psychologists. Pleasure, he adds can never be the end of our strivings; it can only be the accompaniment and consequence of their fulfillment. Frankl's warning that we should be most wary of repressing the *spirit* finds corroboration in the research of Anna Freud. She finds that children produce the deepest of all anxieties not when their desires are repressed, but when their superego or conscience is reduced to the point where they feel unprotected against the pressure of their own drives.[20]

Unchastity is a moral and human defect not because it honors man's sexual instinct but because it divorces instinct from reason, championing the rights of the part at the expense of the integrity of the whole. Chastity demands that sex be humanized, that is to say, integrated into the whole of the human personality. It demands that at times we should abstain from sex; but at the same time, it demands that we never abstain from reason. And it never demands that we abstain from love. Chastity, then, is not simply a negative virtue. "It is," as Dietrich von Hildebrand rightly observes, "a virtue whose positive quality is created by the avoidance of something negative."[21] That something negative is the negation of reason and the failure to integrate the sexual impulse within the totality of the human being. Man is a synthesis. He is not mere sensuousness. Yet he is a synthesis that includes sensuousness, but sensuousness with spirit. And as a synthesis he delights in discovering a life that is enlarged, enabling him to experience his sensuousness—as well as his spirit—more intensely and more abundantly.

The present unpopularity of chastity and its alleged unnaturalness and unlikelihood of attainment are based not nearly so much on the natural power of the sex drive as on the flood of artificial stimulation our aphrodisiac society provides in its tireless atempt to sell everything from toothpaste to town houses. The sexual instinct when left to itself is far less importunate than modern civilization would lead us to think. D.H. Lawrence complained during an era far less saturated with commercial sex than our own that " . . . the mass of our popular literature, the bulk of our popular amusements just exist to provide masturbation."[22] Lawrence bemoaned the fact that the sexual stimuli the entertainment industry provides, fosters and panders to that vast and voracious world of the primitive appetite in the consumer's instinct. Today, the typical mass consumer is a virtual appendage of an exploitive mass media. Marshall McLuhan remarks that "leasing our eyes and ears and nerves to commercial interests is like handing over the common speech to a private corporation, or like giving the earth's atmosphere to a company as a monopoly."[23] Chastity becomes increasingly unlikely to the degree an individual extends himself into mass civilization and the mass media. Chastity is a personal virtue, not a characteristic of our impersonal, commercial world.

The essence of morality is that a person be open to the truth of real things and live by the truth that he grasps. Neither commercial interest nor popular ideology, however, are on the side of the truth of things. To achieve any degree of genuine morality, it seems that an individual must add to the normal task of disciplining his appetites the more demanding one of understanding how he is vulnerable to the various organs of propaganda that invade his environment and how these propaganda mechanisms work. This is a task for which the typical person in our society is very poorly prepared since he tends to trust most of what he sees and hears simply because he does not see or hear anything else. Columnist James Breig states that "TV plots which frequently deal with contraception and abortion and pre- and extra-marital sex should also be grownup enough to deal with chastity, virginity (sans the smirk), and the love of man and woman that surpasses the genitals."[24] But we cannot expect the media to take either a realistic or a balanced view of things. The media by its very nature as a fabricator of discarnate images, is intrinsically unrealistic and unbalanced. Its business is the fictitious and insubstantial world of images, ratings, promotions, profits, success, stardom, jingles, slogans, gimmicks, tricks, replacements, and cancellations. Chastity, because it is a solidly personal value must have its roots in experiences that are substantially personal. In order to promote chastity we must promote experiences that are personal, real, and unmediated. This, in a society of passive spectators—the viewing public and the silent majority—is an extraordinary task and it demands extraordinary efforts from those who discern its worth.

Philosopher Elizabeth Anscombe says that "the trouble about the Christian standard of chastity is that it isn't and never has been generally lived by."[25] We might, strange as it may sound, draw hope from this remark. The contrary would have been cause for great discouragement. For if there ever were a time chastity was generally practiced, it would mean that it was insufficiently inspirational to have been adopted by the succeeding generations. It would seem that if so reasonable and beautiful a virtue as chastity were ever exemplified by the majority of a population, its fire would have continued to flame from generation to generation. It remains for us to help chastity to achieve its long over-due public prominence.

NOTES

[1]Robert Reisner, *Great Wall Writing & Button Grafitti*, (New York: Parallax Publishing Co., 1967), pp. 67,71,77.

[2]C.S. Lewis, *Mere Christianity* (London: Collins, 1961), p. 85.

[3]Aldous Huxley, *Brave New World* (New York: Time, Inc., 1963), p. 208.

On page 207 Huxley writes: "But industrial civilization is only possible when there's no self-denial. Self-indulgence up to the very limits imposed by hygiene and economics. Otherwise the wheels stop turning . . . But chastity means passion, chastity means neurasthenia. And passion and neurasthenia mean instability. And instability means the end of civilization. You can't have a lasting civilization without plenty of pleasant vices."

[4]See Judith Finlayson, "Promiscuity and Celibacy," *Homemaker's Magazine* Jan.-Feb. 1980, p. 44.

[5]Walker Percy, *The Moviegoer* (New York: Popular Library, 1961), p. 204.

[6]For a clear exposition of this point, see Josef Pieper, 'Chastity and Unchastity," *The Four Cardinal Virtues* (New York: Harcourt, Brace & World, 1965). pp. 155-158.

[7]Rollo May, *Love and Will* (New York: Norton, 1969), p. 121.

[8]Aquinas, *Summa Theologica* II-II, Q. 151, Art. 1.

[9]Pieper, *The Four Cardinal Virtues*, p. 160.

[10]T.S. Eliot, "Choruses from 'the Rock'," *The Complete Poems and Plays* (New York: Harcourt, Brace & World, 1952), p. 106.

[11]Berdyaev, *The Destiny of Man* (New York: Harper& Row, 1960), p. 64.

[12]Pieper, p. 161.

[13]C.S. Lewis, p. 89.

[14]Blaise Pascal, *Pascal's Pensées*, tr. by M. Turnell (New Y;ork: Harper & Row, 1962), p. 65.

[15]Constantin von Economo, "Die progressive Zerebration, ein Naturprinzip," Wien. Med. Wschr. 78 (1928): 900-04.

[16]See Josef Roetzer, "Pastoral Medicine and Natural Family Planning," *International Review of Natural Family Planning*, vol. 1, No. 1, summer 1977, pp. 22-30.

[17]Dr. Paul Chaucard, *Maîtrise sexuelle* (Paris, 1959), p. 9. Chaucard speaks of chastity as "triumphing over the temptation to limit one's concept of sex to sexual desire."

[18]Plato, *Republic*, 4. 435-42.

[19]See Cornelius Williams, O.P., "The Hedonism of Aquinas," *The Thomist*, Vol. XXXVIII, April, 1974, p. 261, f.n. 10.

[20]Anna Freud, *Normality and Pathology in Childhood: Assessments of development* (New York: Int. Universities Press, 1965).

[21]Dietrich von Hildebrand, *In Defense of Purity* (New York: Sheed & Ward, 1935), p. 69.

[22]Quoted by Karl Stern in *Love and Success*, p. 107.

[23]Quoted by David Dooley in "Vanishing Moral Codes?", *The Chelsea Journal*, Jan-Feb., p. 12.

[24]James Breig, "TV: The Subtle Seducer," *Liguorian*, March 1980, p. 36.

[25]G.E.M. Anscombe, *Contraception and Chastity* (London: Catholic Truth Society, 1977), p. 24.

11.
Intimacy and the Refusal of Self-Abandonment

> *Man in our day succumbs, in a manner that is not even*
> *perceptible to himself, to alienation from his own humanity*
> *and often, in the name of progress, becomes merely* 'homo
> economicus' *or* 'homo technicus'.
>
> —John Paul II

Intimacy is a closeness between two people that is profoundly personal. Sexual intimacy implies that this closeness includes the possibility of procreating new life. In our society, as social scientists never tire of telling us, people commonly avoid mere involvement with each other, even when involvement is a matter of moral obligation. It should be no surprise, then, that people are even more fearful of intimacy, and hold a special fear of intimacy that is sexual.

The fear of sexual intimacy, therefore, reflects the fear of involvement that characterizes our alienated social situation. Contemporary man is alienated from the fruits of his labor, lacks face-to-face relationships with the people with whom he does business, is a stranger to his own neighbors, and has trouble communicating with members of his own family. His experiences in a milieu of alienation and anonymity provide the blueprint for his sexual relationships, a point that is dramatically expressed in David Susskind's cinematic commentary on the current intimacy problem, *Love and Other Strangers*.

Given the alienating structure of present society, the contraceptive had to come into vogue for it is the symbol of alienation on the level of sexual intercourse that matches and mirrors the general alienation that exists throughout society. Contraception allows sexual partners to go through the motions of being intimate without their being truly intimate, that is, unreservedly and unconditionally so. The fact that contraception is perfectly in accord with the dominant tone of an alienated society means that the general populace scarcely notices its intrusion upon intimacy, although it cannot help but notice the consequences of this intrusion, in the trivialization of sex, the weakening of the marital bond, the increase in infidelity, the decline in the birth rate, and the sharp rise in the rate of married women who conceive and abort unwanted offspring. Contraception also allows intercourse to take place without commitment; and just as Dietrich Bonhoeffer called grace without confession ''cheap grace'', people today speak of intimacy without commitment as ''cheap intimacy.''

The contemporary surrealist painter René Magritte, whose work offers some of the most disturbing images of alienation and fear in the lexicon of modern art, captures the contradiction of non-intimate intimacy in his painting *The Lovers*. Here Magritte portrays a man and a woman posing to kiss each other; but their amorous endeavor is an icon of frustration since their heads are wrapped in gray cloth integuments. They are ''lovers,'' and yet remain anonymous and alienated.[1]

This same insight has been echoed countless times by other artists. C.S. Lewis, in *That Hideous Strength*, describes a form of love-making among a particular tribe of people that represents the logical extreme of marital alienation:

> When a man takes a maiden in marriage, they do not lie together,
> but lie with a cunningly fashioned image of the other, made to move
> and to be warm by devilish arts, for the real flesh will not please them,
> they are so dainty (*delicati*) in their dreams of lust.[2]

Walker Percy carries this theme of alienated love-making even further by completely dissociating the 'lover' from a human partner. In one scene in his novel *Love in the Ruins*, a woman goes to the 'love Clinic' where, attached by Lucite fittings to sensor wires, she is connected to her 'lover' which is a computer.[3]

Commercial advertising, an institution that cannot possibly profit by promoting personal intimacy, offers the contraceptive as being itself the object of love. In one widely circulated ad for condoms the man states that it has the "sensitivity he's looking for", while his female partner approves it because it allows her to feel "protected from pregnancy" What is being affirmed is not the lovers but the condom. Another ad, appearing in a woman's magazine, presents the contraceptive suppository, rather than the man, as the woman's real friend. A popular ad for contraceptive foam describes how "an unnoticeable barrier forms a protective shield between the vagina and the entrance to the womb" and how "male sperm is immobilized instantly upon contact with the foam." The business of contraceptive advertising, of course, is to promote a product, not personal intimacy, and it succeeds only when it convinces people that they are dependent on that product. Personal intimacy, independence, and autonomy are anathema to the contraceptive industry.

Planned Parenthood's single radio commercial warns listeners to "love carefully". The idea that intercourse must be protected by a product is now set to music. Formerly it was believed that love and marriage protected intercourse. Now natural intercourse is regarded as a menace to health and must be protected by contraception. The personal implication is evident: In love-making, the partners should be protected from each other. Natural sexual union is presumed fearful and unprotected. Sexual intimacy is presumed dangerous when it takes place without contraception.

The fact that contraception drives a wedge between sexual partners and alienates individuals from their own sexuality may not be immediately apparent, but it becomes more and more apparent with the passage of time. A newspaper reporter declares in *Viva* magazine: "When I was on the Pill . . . I felt completely cut off from my body and especially from my sexuality."[4] A married woman reports that she had come to detest the intrusion contraception had brought into her relationship with her husband. She expresses the conflict she felt by saying that one action meant "I want to be one with you," while another action meant, "I reject the possible consequences of this oneness."[5] Another woman, described as intelligent, cultured, and internationally traveled, discusses how she suffered mental illness while taking the Pill because of "a schizophrenic division of sexuality from personality."[6] Nona Aguilar has interviewed many individuals whose widely different complaints about contraception could ultimately be reduced to a single complaint: that contraception brings about a profound feeling of alienation between themselves and their partners.[7] Paul Quay had anticipated this split two decades ago when he wrote of the contracepting woman: "She has accepted his affection but not his substance."[8] Five years before *Humanae vitae*, Christopher Derrick reiterated the point when he posed these searing questions:

> Does one show respect for the facts of life if one puts one's seed into a woman while hating, fearing, or resenting the possibility that it might take root in her? Is it either honest or loving to go through the outward motion of surrendering one's sexuality to another person, while taking great care to do nothing of the sort in actual fact?[9]

Sexual intercourse represents pleasure and procreation. Pleasure is universally desirable and requires no special aptitude in order to be enjoyed. Procreation, on the other hand, is undesired more often than not, and understandably since it requires special aptitudes and imposes awesome obligations. The obvious temptation is to separate the two: pleasure from procreation, fun from fertility. The objection is made, however, that such a separation destroys the unity of the sexual act and therefore prevents husband and wife from achieving the kind of intimacy that is appropriate to conjugal lovers. Dietrich von Hildebrand argues that the act of marital intercourse should be one of "perfect self-surrender and self-revelation."[10] Contraception prevents that aspect of self-surrender that could result in new life as well as that aspect of self-revelation that could manifest itself in new parenthood. Contraception always means a compromised unity, a mitigated intimacy. Philosopher Mary Joyce goes so far as to say that the practice of contraception "is a kind of metaphysical schizophrenia or ontological neurosis," tantamount to a denial of the unity of one's own being.[11]

Nonetheless, the notions of less than perfect intimacy and metaphysical disunity seem abstract and academic, whereas contraceptive sex is concrete and undeniable. Those who defend contraception argue that contraceptive sex—compromised intimacy notwithstanding—is much more real as an expression of marital love than disdaining the act for philosophical reasons. Yet this position, compelling as it may be to many, is mounted on two false assumptions: 1) that contraception merely prevents conception; 2) that reality involves only what one immediately experiences.

The fact that two human beings are capable of generation bespeaks a quality of their being and not simply of their generative faculties. It is the father who sires a child not his spermatozoon; it is the mother who gives birth to a baby, not her uterus. To attempt to understand anything in isolation is usually a mistake, but nowhere is it a greater mistake than in the domain of sex. The body is an organism, a concatenation of interdependent cells, tissues, organs, and organ systems. It is a pharmacological axiom that any drug that affects one part of the body, affects another part as well. Moreover, the body and the soul are unitary. What affects one affects the other. Contraception does much more than prevent conception; it violates the integrity of the sex act as well as the body-spirit integrity of the partners. As one writer expresses it, contraception "tears at the marvelous web of love spinning itself into life and destroys the sexual ecstasy and therefore the wholeness of marriage."[12] Such thinking helps to explain the innumerable psychological and physiological adverse side effects that all forms of contraception from the condom to the Copper-T routinely produce. Many argue that the contraceptive side effects are offset by the side effects that would otherwise be produced by pregnancy. Yet this argument falsely assumes that there is no alternative natural form of birth control that would be both effective and risk free. More importantly, it falsely assumes that the wholly unnecessary risks of sterile sex can equitably be compared with the risks that attend procreative intercourse that results in new life and ensures the continuance of the human species.

The second assumption, which regards intimacy as an "ideal" and man's being as an "abstraction", is essentially unrealistic. What happens to man on the level of his being may not impress itself on his consciousness immediately, but it is nonetheless there as a *real* part of him and will make itself known sooner or later, one way or another, consciously or unconsciously. Cardinal Suenens says that "contraception is an essential denial of conjugal communion, which it secretly disintegrates and turns into deceit and self-seeking."[13] The ill effects of contraception may exist secretly at first, but, as many have learned through painful experience, they make their presence felt in due time. The hazards of the Pill are particularly well documented.[14] In one British study nearly ten percent of the women taking oral contraceptives became mentally depressed, sometimes to the point of requiring psychiatric treatment.[15] A North Carolina study reported that the oral contraceptive may produce severe emotional disturbances in women ranging from irritability to marked depression with suicidal thought (suicide has been reported to the Federal Drug Administration as a side-effect of the Pill). Adverse reactions were noted anywhere from one week to six months after therapy started.[16] Barbara Seaman, author of *The Doctor's Case Against the Pill*, remarks that the Pill produces a depression in some women that builds up slowly and gets worse with each cycle.

The attempt by chemical or mechanical means to separate intercourse from procreation represents a fractionalization of the marriage act and the partners themselves. It is like asking for only the sweet smelling flower but not the sharp thorns, the deep roots, or the hot sun. But the flower needs the thorns for protection, the roots for nourishment, and the sun for color. Contraception represents an unrealistic request to excoriate sexual pleasure from its inviolable, health-giving context of wholeness and intimacy.

Uncompromised sexual intimacy is not merely a worthy ideal; it is the immediate obligation of any married couple who wants to be and remain a married couple. The fact of the matter is that marital intimacy is usually compromised not for the sake of a better love relationship, but so that one's intimacy with something else is not compromised. Protestant historian Jeremy Jackson points out that "the tendency for Christians' reasons for contraception and abortion to match is a function of their underlying desire for material security."[17] Charles E. Curran, hardly a traditionalist on the subject of contraception, warns how it could easily enclose man in the realm of the purely material.[18] A married couple may decide to compromise their sexual intimacy by using contraception because they do not want to compromise their standard of living, their social status, their job security, or their savings. Their real unity is with something socio-economic.

Dr. John Schimel reports the dream of one of his patients:

> I am in bed with my wife, and between us is my accountant. He is going to have intercourse with her. My feeling about this is odd—only that somehow it seemed appropriate.[19]

This dream strongly suggests two things: the man's alienation from his wife, whose concern for material security (symbolized by her sexual union with the accountant) is greater than her concern for him; that his disunified marriage is his own doing since he gave the accountant too important a role in his marriage (this is why he views the situation as "appropriate"). Dr. Schimel, who has dealt with many patients whose sexual relationships suffer from a lack of intimacy, observes that his patients "have endured stoically, without noticing, remarkably destructive treatment at the hands of their spouses, but they have experienced falling behind in the sexual time-table as a loss of love."[20] Schimel is alluding to the fact that his patients, having abandoned intimacy concerns, become preoccupied—if not with material security, as in the case of the dreamer—with technique or performance. Excessive concern for performance, needless to say, inclines the individual to think too much about himself as a performer, a fact that naturally militates against his intimacy with another. Schimel discusses a particular patient whose concern for his own performace led him to the point where he applied an anesthetic ointment to himself before engaging in intercourse. He was willing to pay the price of reducing his feeling of union with his partner (as well as his own pleasure) in order to improve his performance. Such a self-defeating pattern inevitably led to his impotence.

Rollo May speaks of the peculiar progression from an "anesthetic" attitude toward sex wherein people feel less and less pleasure to an "antiseptic" one in which sexual contact "tends to get put on the shelf and avoided."[21] The next step is a new asceticism which is more negatively disposed toward sex than was the old puritanism. The *Hite Report* offers the personal testimonies of many individuals who, finding promiscuous and sterile sex disillusioning, turned to the new celibacy for relief. Columbia University psychiatrist Joel Joskowitz refers to this phenomenon as "secondary virginity".[22]

Extreme and unnatural concern for technical performance is consistent with sex as a form of professional entertainment. The purpose of pornography is not for the participants, but for the spectators. The requirement of pornography that it have observers, of course, is in direct contradiction to the requirements of intimacy.[23] Intimacy belongs to the spiritual order and its expression, being intimate, is neither repeatable nor discloseable. Pornography, because of its primary concern for performance, is directed to the eye, and to a public of strangers.

As sexual intimacy is compromised through contraception, an

inevitable movement begins whose intrinsic tendency is dangerous because it allows partners to establish a more inviolable union with something other than each other, such as material security or personal convenience. This tendency reaches its most advanced stages of alienation in the various forms of pornography, that abound in our present culture. It is worth noting that sex counselors often recommend pornographic films, books, and magazines to married couples who complain that their sex life has lost some of its luster. Contraception and pornography belong to the same tendency, a tendency that moves away from intimacy. Brent Bozell, appearing on the Dick Cavett show, went so far as to state that contraception in fact is pornography. At any rate, there can be no doubt that the contraceptive, so suited to an alienated society, has played an important role in directing people further and further away from intimacy. It is fitting, therefore, that James Reed would title his work on the history of the birth control movement and American society since 1830 as *From Private Vice to Public Virtue*.[24] Sexual intercourse used to be a private act that had a public implication; now it is seen as a public act that has a private implication.

The Old Testament Hebrews used the word *yadoah* ("to know") for the act of sexual union. Knowledge and sexual love have an important factor in common in that they both imply an entering into something that exists outside of the self. The knower is united with the object of his knowledge and his knowledge is objective to the degree it is free from subjective prejudices and biases. The true knower knows his object as that object is and not as the knower might prefer it to be. Likewise, the true lover will love his partner as she is, without altering her being to suit some convenience or security need. In the same sense, the ancients held that "ubi amor, ibi oculus"—where there is love, there is also vision (knowledge).

The Greeks spoke of "scotosis", an intellectual blindness that inhibits a man from knowing certain things he is afraid of knowing. Modern psychologists speak of a subject's selective blindness or deafness that prevents him from acknowledging the existence of realities that are too painful for him to acknowledge. This condition is the cognitive equivalent of the contraceptive that blocks out conception. It is no mere accident that the word "conception" applies to the mind as well as to the uterus. A man who suffers from "scotosis" would be considered a poor scholar.

One who chooses "scotosis" as a way of improving his mind would be regarded as something of a fanatic.

In knowing and loving taken together—*yadoah*—a special intimacy is achieved between husband and wife in which each knows and loves the other with reverence, that is, with respect for the way they are. Contraception represents a fear of this *yadoah* intimacy. It is a way by which man and woman know and love not each other, exactly, but something different, something more convenient, less fearful. The problem of contraception in our society is compounded by the fact that the popular attitude toward it is itself contracepted, in the cognitive sense, because the truth of contraception is too painful for most people to acknowledge. Thus, there exists widespread *philosophical* contraception.

Intimacy requires knowledge and love in the strictest sense of these terms. But knowledge and love need courage and courage needs faith. If there should be one sacrosanct, uncompromisable, intimate relationship between people in all of society it should be the sexual union between husband and wife. Marriage, then, demands extraordinary and well-developed abilities. Accordingly, one German writer states that "marriage is the hallowed ground, the sanctified place for those lovers who should, who are able, who are permitted and who are determined to take the risk of procreation."[25] Marital intimacy is difficult and menaced on all sides. Yet its difficulties pale when compared with its rewards: for it is the antidote *par excellence* for loneliness, selfishness, fear, and alienation; and it is the ordinary and unsurpassable means of conceiving new life, and by virtue of that new life offering a weary world new hope.

NOTES

[1]Robert Hughes, "Enter the Stolid Enchanger: a René Magritte retrospective," *Time*, March 5, 1979, p. 66.

[2]C.S. Lewis, *That Hideous Strength* (London: Pan Books, 1961), p. 166-7.

[3]Walker Percy, *Love in the Ruins* (New York: Dell, 1972), p. 118.

[4]Lionel Tiger, "The Emotional Effects of the Pill," *Viva*, 1974. p. 44.

[5]Larry and Nordis Christenson, "Contraception: Blessing or Blight?" *The Christian Couple* (Minneapolis: Bethany Fellowship, 1977).

[6]Christenson.

[7]Nona Aguilar, *No-Pill, No-Risk Birth Control* (New York: Rawson, Wade, 1980). In many cases the emotional split caused by the use of contraception led

to separation or divorce.

[8]Paul Quay,S.J., "Contraception and Conjugal Love," *Theological Studies*, Vol. 22, 1961, p. 35. See also Stanislas de Lestapis, S.J., *La limitation des naissances* (Paris, 1958), p. 183.

[9]Christopher Derrick, "From the 'Spectator,' 20 September 1963," *The Pill and Birth Regulation*, ed Leo Pyle (Helicon: Baltimore, 1964), p. 55.

[10]Dietrich von Hildebrand, *In Defense of Purity* (New York: Helicon, 1931), p. 36.

[11]Mary Rosera Joyce, *The Meaning of Contraception* (New York: Helicon, 1931), p. 36.

[12]Patrick Gavan-Duffy Riley, "The Wholeness of Marriage," *Homiletic and Pastoral Review*, June, 1968, p. 751.

[13]Leon Joseph Cardinal Suenens, *Love and Control* (Westminster, Md.: Newman, 1964), p. 103.

[14]For a thorough analysis of the medical hazards of the Pill see Herbert Ratner, M.D. "The Medical Hazards of the Birth Control Pill," *Child & Family Quarterly*, rpt. Dec. 1969.

[15]Brenda Herzberg, M.D. (Medical Research Council, England), "Oral Contraceptives and Depression," *Medical World News*, Jan. 5, 1968.

[16]Francis Kane, Jr. M.D. et al, "Psychological Effects of Oral Contraceptives," American Psychiatric Association 121 Annual Meeting 1965, *Medical Tribune*, May 26, 1965. In the *British Medical Journal* of September 15, 1979, Valerie Beral, a lecturer in epidemiology and medical statistics writes: "The transfer from traditional to modern methods of birth control, during the past 25 years, has been accompanied by a transfer of deaths from complications of pregnancy to death from complications of modern contraceptive methods. . . It is estimated that in 1975 more women aged 25-44 years died from adverse effects of the pill, than from all complications of pregnancy combined (including abortion) . . . in 1975 there may well have been more than seven times as many pill-related deaths as pregnancy-related deaths in women aged 35-44 years."

[17]Jeremy C. Jackson, "The Shadow of Death: Abortion in Historical and Contemporary Perspective," *Thou Shalt Not Kill*, ed. Richard L. Ganz (New Rochelle: Arlington House, 1978), p. 94.

[18]Charles E. Curran, "Personal Reflections on Birth Control," *The Catholic Case for Contraception*, ed. Daniel Callahan (London: Macmillan, 1969), p. 19.

[19]Dr. John Schimel, as quoted in Rollo May, *Love and Will* (New York: Norton, 1969), p. 38.

[20]John L. Schimel, "Ideology and Sexual Practices," *Sexual Behavior and the Law*, ed. Ralph Slovenko (Springfield, Ill.: Charles Thomas, 1965), pp. 195-197.

[21]May, p. 61.

[22]"The Embarrassed Virgins," *Time*, July 9, 1973, p. 46.

[23]See Michael Joseph Sobran, "Pornography," *The Human Life Review*, Summer, 1977, p. 84. "The 'lovers' in a pornographic film aim to gratify not themselves or each other, but the spectator, with whom they are in fact perform-

ing an unnatural sex act.''

[24]James Reed, *From Private Vice to Public Virtue* (New York: Basic Books, 1978).

[25]Ida Friederike Gorres, *Zwischen den Zeiten* (Olten: Walter, 1961), p. 64.

12.
Fidelity and the Terror of Irreversibility

Like frog's legs, swinging can be continued, dropped, or practiced in moderation or abundance once tried.
—Caroline Gordon

Whenever an aspect of daily life is no longer integrated into the rhythm of existence, it draws disproportionate attention to itself. Ordinarily we do not pay much attention to our drinking water, but if suddenly we are informed that it is contaminated, it becomes the central topic of conversation for our whole community. Likewise, I do not spend much time thinking about my teeth unless I have a toothache, when I can think of little else.

In the Western world a disproportionate amount of attention is given to sex. This attention, in itself, is symptomatic of a cultural failure to integrate sex into the whole of human existence. Commercial advertising, the entertainment industry, popular conversation, school curricula, and the extraordinary proliferation of sex magazines offer abundant indication that non-integrated sex is a major cultural preoccupation. People have "sex on the brain," comments Malcolm Muggeridge, and "that's an unhealthy place for it to be." Philosopher Henri Bergson has charged that "sex-appeal is the keynote of our whole civilization."[1] Indeed, it is often regarded as a *summum bonum*. "All ambition leads to the bedroom," states today's sophisticated citizen of the post-Freudian era. Existentialist psychologist Adrian van Kaam writes, "Because man's attention is drawn so concentratedly to sex, we suspect that it does not fit smoothly into the totality of his existence."[2]

As interest in sex increases and intensfies, social critics express their astonishment that a "saturation point" has not already been reached. The real wonder, however, is that virtual "saturation" and "sex starvation" can exist side by side. One is uncomfortably reminded of the plight of the Ancient Mariner. "Water, water, every where, / Nor any drop to drink."[3]

Our society (and therefore our thinking) is dominated by science and all the presuppositions that belong to a purely scientific methodology. One basic characteristic of a purely scientific approach is to be analytic, that is to reduce things to their parts and then seek the meaning of the whole in terms of the functioning of the parts. The abiding motive behind the 2,000-year-old "search for the atom" is precisely a desire to understand the nature of the whole by knowing the functioning of its elementary and constitutive parts.

The great success of science in modern times has been evidenced through technology. During this time two great industrial revolutions have taken place: the first, which substituted mechanical energy for living energy (that of animals and men); the second, which substituted computers for human thinking. The genius of science and technolgy, then, has been to mechanize life.

The great cultural philosopher Lewis Mumford maintains that the central phenomenon that connects the past with the future is what he calls the "megamachine"[4] The "megamachine" is the "totally organized and homogenized social system in which society as such functions like a machine and men like its parts."[55] Thus, the Cartesian *Cogito* which inaugurated the era of modern science and philosophy receives its ultimate expression in the form of fragmented man, who announces: "*Cog ergo Sum.*"[6]

The machine has not only renewed the face of the earth but, more important, has become the central analogy by which modern man understands himself and the nature of life. Biologist Ludwig von Beralanffy contends, "The acceptance of living beings as machines, the domination of the modern world by technology, and the mechanization of mankind are but the extension and practical application of the mechanistic conception of physics."[7] Social critic Floyd Matson argues that the human world has become "mechanomorphized"; the human "subject" is now regarded as scientific "object."[8]

Thus, society has become fragmented into an assortment of mechanical parts, and in the process man has become de-spiritualized and de-individualized. In the name of efficiency and bureaucratic control, modern man submits to the forces in fashion and allows his indivduality to be reduced to quantifiable units and his personality to something that can be expressed on punched cards.[9]

Bureaucracy, automation, megamachine, functionary, consumer, corporation man, organization man—all are terms which remind us of the fragmented condition of our contemporary life, of how, in the day-to-day routine of things, we are made to feel less than whole.[10] Cubism portrays this phenomenon with merciless candor. "In Picasso's pictures we feel the real pain of the world's coming apart, layer by layer, the world's dematerialization and decrystallization, the atomization of the world's flesh, the rending of all the veils."[11]

In a fragmented society it is inevitable that human relationships become fragmentary. And the most prevalent form of such relationships is sexual. The reason is that sex is rooted in man's inescapable biology and is, as Rollo May puts it, the "lowest common denominator on the ladder of salvation."[12]

A fundamental feature of a fragmented sexual relationship is an obsessive preoccupation with parts, that is, with the genitals and other erotogenic areas.[13] In this regard the human body is represented as a machine,[14] one that will be in good running order when its key parts are functioning well. Certain words that refer to automobile parts have been extended to apply to "parts" of the female anatomy. One automobile advertisement compares a woman's "vital statistics" with the three important features people are looking for in an economy car—highway, city, and average miles per gallon.[15]

At times a sexual relationship can be so fragmentary as to impede a personal recognition. In Eugene Ionesco's *The Bald Soprano* two people meet and, through a protracted conversation that reveals a number of striking coincidences, discover that they are man and wife. The movie *John and Mary* (Dustin Hoffman and Mia Farrow) closes when two lovers ask each other's names. Their laconic replies—"Mary," "John"—more than suggest they are still personal strangers to each other. "What makes a gal a good number?" The simple answer is "looking like a number of other gals."[16] In the mechanization of human relationships, numbers replace names. As the song says, "When I'm not near the girl I love, I love the girl I'm near."[17]

In the impersonal, anti-utopian world of Orwell's *Nineteen Eighty-Four*, two central characters insist that their sexual affair be subpersonal. Winston asks, "You like doing this? I don't mean simply me: I mean the thing in itself?" Julia replies, "I adore it." "That was above all what he wanted to hear. Not merely the love of one person but the animal instinct, the simple undifferentiated desire."[18]

At other times sexual relationships are fragmented to the point of actually eliminating the human partner altogether. One popular magazine whose monthly sales are well into the millions has advertised "Judy— the Instant girlfriend: her skin is a warm flesh-like vinyl that makes humans almost robotic"[19] In an ad for condoms that has appeared and reappeared in a Canadian national weekly, an attractive young woman says: "My Man is a Shield's Man." The ad explains that this particular brand of condom is the true object of love for both the man and the woman.

Fragmentary sexual relationships must always be disappointing, because they are based on a distorted view of man. Thus, they are alway antagonistic to his deepest, most personal needs. The view that sex is a specific function of man, having to do with certain parts of his anatomy, is not based on an understanding of man's nature but is the result of society's acceptance of the machine as the single, universal metaphor by which all of nature is understood.

The machine dominates our consciousness because science and technology are the prevailing dominant forces in our culture. The current problem concerning sex devolves upon the difficulty in seeing forms of wholeness in a society where the overwhelming tendency is to view everything analytically in terms of its component parts.

The great critic of science, Henri Bergson, has discussed this problem in terms of the natural opposition that exists between intelligence and intuition, that is, between the faculty that analyzes the parts and the one that enjoys a sympathetic view of the whole. He writes: "From intuition one can pass to analysis, but not from analysis to intuition."[20] It is of paramount importance, then, that before we analyze we know what it is we are analyzing. We know a thing in its wholeness directly and intuitively. We cannot know the wholeness or the nature of anything by adding up its component parts.

The modern view of sex, then, is the result of the exclusive operation of the intelligence on matter rather than a direct intuition of the person. As a consequence, our fragmentary view of man and sex leads to frustrating and unfulfilling relationships.[21]

Sex is wholly connected with personality, and man's nature as a sexual being is grasped not by analysis but by intuition. Thus, a proper sexual relationship is interpersonal, expressing itself by a desire to *be with* the other rather than reduce the other to a sexual accessory or a commodity or a fragment of what he is in his wholeness.[22]

Sex that is fragmented is motivated not by love but by lust. And since lust is not an attribute of the whole person, its expression cannot result in any of those experiences—especially joy—that belong to the person as such. Kurt Goldstein states in his work *Human Nature in the Light of Psychopathology* that "the hedonistic tendency originates in the abnormal isolation of one attribute of human nature. . . . In consequence he [the hedonist] is incapable of experiencing the positive character of joy."[23] In other words, when sex is regarded as a part of the person it cannot provide for experiences that belong to the whole of the person. Therefore, those who look for joy in fragmented sex are always disappointed.[24]

Similarly, Berdyaev states: "The lust of sensuality is joyless and is not really a passion: it belongs to a realm in which the primary passion, ontological in its significance, has cooled down and been replaced by fictitious passions which condemn man to the bad infinity of insatiable longing.[25]

Many people identify the process of aging with the process of dying. As the poet Ernest Dowson laments, "To grow is to lose." In a certain elementary sense that it true. The child, Freud held, is "polymorphous." There are so many directions that are open to him. He is a kind of inifinitude of possibilities.

> How many things rise up in the vision of a mother as she gazes in wonder upon her little one? Illusion perphaps! This is not certain. Let us rather say that reality is big with possibilities, and that the mother sees in the child not only what he will become, but also what he would become, if he were not obliged, at every step in his life, to choose

and therefore exclude.[26]

As we grow and as we choose our specific course of life, our number of possible choices ever diminishes. "Growing," as psychiatrist Karl Stern expresses it, "means *an increase of the irreversible*, of the fact that more and more doors get *locked behind us* as we advance."[27]

Most choices that we make, no matter how securely they seal us from our past, do not affect us in any significant way. However, in those areas that involve our whole being, the matter can be quite different. Psychoanalysts know well that the panic experienced on the eve of one's wedding (which sometimes leads to calling off the marriage) is relatable to a fear of death.[28] Marriage represents a "letting go" or dying to the past and a commitment to a new but uncertain future. We feel a sense of the irreversible whenever we make choices and commitments that are of a sexual nature involving our whole being. The concept of marital fidelity—of remaining faithful to one's spouse—can appear severely limiting. At the same time, a return to the infantile world of no commitment and infinite choice can seem eminently desirable. Because such a desire is essentially regressive it is sometimes identified as a desire to return to the womb. The tendency not to "let go," to hold on to the past, is also a refusal to grow as a person.

One is stricken with a "terror of the irreversible" when he senses that his life is getting smaller, that the best part of his life is irrevocably behind him. In such a state he may make a desperate bid to regain the suppleness and potential of his earlier life by engaging in a multiplicity of sexual adventures with a variety of partners. However, such escapades are necessarily selfish and fragmentary. They are also unrealistic in the sense that they treat fragmentary sexual relationships as if they were man's highest good, the all-sufficient object of his being. In a similar vein, Max Weber has analyzed the excesses of capitalism in terms of a mad drive for the self-sufficient.[29]

The plight of the person who seeks meaning in life through promiscuity is analogous to the drowning man who clutches anything near him, a twig or a leaf, in a desperate attempt to remain afloat. But to use (in the sense of exploit) people sexually as a means of creating meaning for one's existence is the very essence of perversity.[30]

In an extraordinary passage in Nabokov's *Lolita*, Humbard, who is terrified of aging and of losing Lolita to younger men, entertains a mad fantasy. He dreams of using his twelve-year-old partner to give him Lolita II and then that daughter to give him Lolita III. Thus, through a perverse, incestuous pattern he will hold off the aging process of his sex mate and exempt himself, in one small way, from the march of the irreversible.[31] Here the irreversible is linked with death, and Humbard's fear of death is so acute that it prevents him from concentrating his energies on living life.

Every choice is an exclusion. If I choose one wife I exclude, by that same choice, all other potential wives. Yet I do not feel cheated by such an arrangement, for one actual wife is superior to any number of possible wives. Choice does not reduce a person to less than what he is, especially when his choice is the fruition of his love. The perpetually indecisive person, like Prufrock,[32] is not happy with his unclaimed infinitude of possibilites; by refraining from choosing, he refrains from living. Chesterton puts it thus:

> Every act of the will is an act of self-limitation. To desire action is
> to desire limitation. In that sense every act is an act of self-sacrifice.
> When you choose anything, you reject everything else.[33]

Modern man wants, simultaneously, what he chooses and what his choice rejects. Infidelity is a form of trying to choose without excluding. It is often, in reality, symptomatic of not choosing at all.

Marriage involves maintaining a proper balance between "having" and "holding". Don Juan wants to "*have*" all women but, in so attempting the impossible, cannot "hold" any one in particular. Humbard desires to "hold" on to Lolita so fiercely that he is tempted to devour her, thus making it impossible for him to "have" her.[34] One must "let go" of his "hold" on his loved one to give her room to be. And yet if he "has" (that is, sexually) more than one, he runs the risk of not "holding" the one he loves. His "having" affords knowledge and intimacy, whereas his "holding" gives centrality to his married life. Infidelity betrays intimacy and disrupts centrality while moving in the direction of the casual, fragmentary affairs that have little or no existential meaning.

Reluctance to accept the reality that exclusion is the natural concomitant of choice is an indication that there was little will or love behind the choice. In a very real sense to choose to live is to choose to die. "In every choice we must die."[35] But we do not live and die to the same thing. We live to what we need ("need" taken in the deepest sense), and we die to or "let go of" what we do not need. But we must first learn what it is that we need and what it is that we do not need. Then we may find the love that casts out fear, so that our love for what we need is stronger than our fear of losing what we do not need. In this context, the fear of being "bound"[36] or the terror of the irreversible is irrelevant, and what is central is a sense of personal growth that is characterized by a purifying of who we are and the rightfulness of our destiny.

"To complain that I could only be married once," remarks Chesterton, "was like complaining that I had only been born once."[37] Given the parameters of existence—of life and death, choice and exclusion—monogamy and fidelity make sense because they offer centrality and direction. And since each of us is only one, we need but one center and one destination. The movement from a love of what answers our deepest needs to a fascination with a multitude of possibilities is regressive, as I have stated above. But it is also, as a negation of our proper destiny and our true freedom, a choice for anonymity and necessity. Being unlimited but not being myself is not a state of personal freedom. It is the state of the primitive—not yet free. On the other hand, accepting my limitations and finding my proper destiny therein is the essence of freedom. Ortega y Gasset remarks: "We have to seek in our circumstances just as it is, *precisely in its quality as limitation*, as peculiarity, the right place in the immense perspective of the world. In short, the reabsorption of circumstance is the concrete destiny of man.[38]

Fidelity has a threefold implication. First, marital fidelity affirms the wholeness of a spousal relationship and, by excluding its opposite, gives centrality to married life. Second, fidelity applies to the relationship one has with his destiny.[39] The positive element involves choosing what one needs in order to become himself; negatively, by excluding its opposite, one avoids the slide into personal inauthenticity. Third, fidelity means the consistent choice of God.

Aristotle wrote in his *Politics* that "it is the nature of desire to be infinite." Two millenia later Nietzsche echoed the same insight when he exclaimed, "All desire demands infinity."[40] In our limited lives we cannot choose an infinite number of things. Dr. Faustus, Don Juan, and the compulsive consumer are images of restlessness and frustration. It is hopeless to seek infinity in the form of accumulation. Moreover, it is equally hopeless to seek the infinite in the finite as such. The philosopher Benedetto Croce states: "The impressionable, sentimental and fickle minds, having lost sight of the true God made to themselves idols. . . . They identified the infinite with this or that finite, the ideal with this or that perceptible."[41]

Fidelity—and, ultimately, fidelity to God—solves the paradox of finite man who is the subject of infinite longing. God alone is infinite. Thus, man can satisfy his desire for the infinite only in God. Yet man works out his life in a context where the wide variety of all his choices involves the finite and the tangible.

There are times in a person's life, as I have mentioned, when his fear of the irreversible prevents him from making a commitment to another. At these times he has a sense that something on the level of his *being* must die. Thus, a man might be reluctant to accept marital fidelity because, in foregoing sex with others, he would forfeit experiences that would involve him on the level of his being. And yet, by abandoning fidelity one is faced with a loss of centrality and a sequence of fragmentary affairs that neither have meaning nor satisfy his desire for the infinite. Commenting on Gabriel Marcel's notion of "creative fidelity", scholar James Collins writes; "What Thomas Hardy called man's unhope is the outcome of refusing to extend credit to the universe in the direction of its transcendent source. And the fruit of unhope is despair."[42]

Fidelity requires that we die to all the relationships and material possessions we could merely "have" so that we can purify our own being and at the same time move in the direction of infinite being. We move back to the infinite source of being by remaining faithful to its image in us—our own being. By remaining faithful with the one with whom we are sexually united, and faithful to our proper destiny, we adopt existential patterns that are consistent with our being and our faithfulness with God. That is why Berdyaev can say: "From the spiritually mystical point of view 'infidelity' is terrible, for it is the betrayal of the eternal to the temporal, the victory of death over life,"[43] and why Marcel can say: "A code of ethics centered on fidelity is irresistibly led to become attached to what is more than human, to a desire for the unconditional which is the requirement and the very mark of the absolute in us."[44]

Unless we are willing to die to what we do not need, we will die altogether. Life is a process of stripping away the things that distract us from our destiny with the Divine. The process, to be sure, is accompanied by suffering. In an affluent society the social reflex is well established, that a convenient anodyne be applied at the first sign of suffering. Alcohol, sex, and entertainment are all readily accesible narcotics that are designed to distract us from our faithful commitment to what we really need.[45] But the way we face our anxieties is also the way we face our death. By accepting death and difficulty, sorrow and suffering, in the interest of fidelity to a higher love, we experience a release from the order of the absurd and the necessary, and begin to understand the-meaning of our life and the warmth of God's love. Karl Stern adds, "In order to accept death truly I must abandon all I *have* (not only in material property) in order to face the infinite *being*, God, who is at the same time infinite love.

Sex is a form through which man may become united with God. However, in a culture whose tone is predominantly scientific-analytic, a strong tendency exists to segregate sex from the whole of man's personality and view it as if it were something in and by itself. Fragmentary sexual relationships thus abound, but they are not satisfying nor can they provide joy, since, they are not grounded in the whole of man's being.

A sexual relationship that is fully personal and "being-to-being" demands fidelity; for fidelity alone by carefully balancing the polarities of "have" and "hold," can afford centrality and meaning to one's sexual life and at the same time safeguard against the dissipating and frustrating conequences of exploitive "having" and possessive "holding." Fidelity is a profoundly wise tradition; there is also much wisdom in the ancient saying that if you allow Venus to have her way she will lead you to Mars. Fidelity redeems instinct through reason and love.

When man is faithful to the implications of his being, particularly those of his sexuality and personal destiny, he is in harmony with God, the source of all being. Moreoover, man's desire is infinite, and thus neither individual finite objects nor any accumulation of them can satisfy him. Thus, his ultimate fidelity is with God, who is infinite being.

When man places his stake in the finite, he is often stricken with a "terror of the irreversible" when he senses that his choices are becoming fewer and his life shorter. To the man who loves God, dying to what separates him from God is not problematic. Thus, man's attitude toward sex, fidelity, and God turns on his disposition toward love, life, and death. In this regard, a philosophy of being, together with psychological insights and poetic intuition into man and the nature of human existence, is in full accord with the scriptural statements "He who would save his life will lose it,"[47] "Without Me you can do nothing"[47] and "He who does the truth comes to the light."[49]

NOTES

[1]Henri Bergson, *The Two Sources of Morality and Religion* (Garden City: Doubleday, 1935), p. 302.

[2]Adrian van Kaam, "Sex and Existence," *Review of Existential Psychology and Psychiatry*, vol. 3, no. 2 (May 1963).

[3]Samuel Taylor Coleridge, *The Rime of the Ancient Mariner*, II, ll. 121-22.

[4]Lewis Mumford, *The Myth of the Machine* (New York: Harcourt, Brace, Jovanovich, 1970),

[5]Erich Fromm, *The Revolution of Hope* (New York: Harcourt, Brace, Jovanovich, 1970).

[6]Philospher John H. Randall states that Descartes made of nature "a machine and nothing but a machine; purposes and spiritual significance had alike been banished. . . . Intoxicated by his vision and his success, he boasted, 'Give me extension and motion, and I will construct the universe.' " *The Making of the Modern Mind* (Boston: Houghton MIfflin, 1940), pp. 241-242. Erich Fromm writes: "Man, as cog in the production machine, becomes a thing, and ceases to be human," *The Revolution of Hope*, p. 38.

[7]Ludwig Bertalanffy, *Problems of Life* (New York: Harper Torchbooks, 1960), p. 202.

[8]Floyd Matson, *The Broken Image* (New York: Doubleday, 1966), p. 231.

[9]C.S. Lewis writes: "Perhaps in the nature of things, analytic understanding must always be a basilisk which kills what it sees and only sees by killing." *The Abolition of Man* (New York: Macmillan, 1947), p. 90.

[10]Consider these images from Thomas Pynchon's novel, V (New York; Bantam 1963): "Turn a corner . . . and there he'd be, in alien country." Or else he'd be "walking the aisles of a bright, gigantic supermarket, his only function to want."

[11]Nicolas Berdyaev, *The Meaning of the Creative Act* (New York: Collier,

1962), p. 225. Cf. Rollo May, *Love and Will* (New York: Norton, 1969), p. 23: "Or in Picasso . . . whose insight into the schizoid character of our modern world is seen in the fragmented bulls and torn villagers in *Guernica*, or in the distorted portraits with mislocated eyes and ears—paintings not named but numbered."

[12]May, *Love and Will*, p. 14: Sex "seems always dependable to give at least a facsimile of love."

[13]Cf. George Frankl, *The Failure of the Sexual Revolution* (New York: Humanities, 1974), p. 129: "One of the important aspects of depersonalised or dissociated sex is that it is preoccupied with part objects. The erotic zones become separated from the personality, and the whole process of love, affection and desire is reduced to the preoccupation with genitals and other erotogenic zones."

[14]May, *Love and Will*, p. 47: "Sex becomes our tool like the caveman's bow and arrows, crowbar, or adz. Sex, the new machine, the *Michina Ultima*."

[15]This newspaper ad for the Chevette Scooter brought considerable notoriety: "40 EPA Hwy mpg (built not to bust); 28 EPA City mpg (Pinches waste in every way); 33 EPA Average PG (Very hip in looks)."

[16]Herbert Marshall McLuhan, *The Mechanical Bride* (New York: Vanguard Press, 1951), p. 96: " 'What's the trick that makes her click?' The answer is 'being a replaceable part.' "

[17]From the Broadway musical *Guys and Dolls*.

[18]George Orwell, (New York: New American Library, 1949), p. 103. Cf. also Lewis Mumford, *The Condition of Man* (New York: Harcourt, Brace Jovanovich, 1973), p. 243: "The people who are honored as benefactors of the race in (Bacon's) fragmentary utopia *The New Atlantis*, are all scientists or inventors of the practical arts. . . . Feelings, emotions, states of mind, were becoming unreal to him and his scientifically minded contemporaries; they faced the perils of subjective hallucination by closing up that side of the personality and declaring it utterly bankrupt."

[19]Cited in Frankl, *The Failure of the Sexual Revolution*, pp. 111,115.

[20]Henri Bergson, *An Introduction to Metaphysics* (Indianapolis: Bobbs-Merrill, 1903), p. 42.

[21]Cf. Nicholas Berdyaev, *The Destiny of Man* (New York: Harper Torchbooks, 1955). p. 61: "Sex is not a function of the human organism but a quality of it as a whole and of every cell which composes it." Whatever it was that Masters and Johnson measured when they observed 694 people (382 women and 312 men) during more than 10,000 cycles of sexual excitation, it had nothing to do with personality, sexual wholeness, or effect of interpersonal love such as joy, spiritual communion, and so on.

[22]Cf. Karl Barth's notion of *Mitmensch*, co-humanity, in *Church Dogmatics* (Naperville, Ill.: Allenson, 1957), ll, 2.

[23]Kurt Goldstein, *Human Nature in the Light of Psychopathology* (New York: Shocken, 1940), p. 228.

[24]The eternal cry of such sexual unfulfillment is heard from Ovid's "*Post*

coitum omne animal triste est" to the Rolling Stones' "I can't get no satisfaction."

[25]Berdyaev, *The Destiny of Man*, p. 183.

[26]Bergson, *The Two Sources of Morality and Religion*, p. 45.

[27]Karl Stern, *Love and Success* (New York: Farrar, Straus & Giroux, 1952), p. 89.

[28]Stern, "Death within Life," *Review of Existential Psychology and Psychiatry*, vol 2 (1962), pp. 141-44.

[29]Cf. Hanna Colm, "The Demonic in Love and Sex," *Review of Existential Psychology and Psychiatry*, vol. 3 (1963). The author states: "With this rationalistic drive man lost the feeling of his human dependency on the 'Ground of Being' and on something as irrational as Grace."

[30] Van Kaam, "Sex and Existence": Perversity means a fixation on sexual modes of existence which are incompatible with a wholesome project of life. Perversion indicates a fixated disintegration of sex and existence."

[31]Vladimir Nabokov, *Lolita* (New York: Putnam, 1955), p. 176. P. 67: "The word 'forever' referred only to my own passion, to the eternal Lolita as reflected in my blood."

[32]T.S. Eliot, "The Love Song of J. Alfred Prufrock" in *Collected Works* (New York: Harcourt, Brace, Jovanovich, 1963). Prufrock is the image of the contemporary catatonic who fears love, choice, and life to the point where he tumbles into death. "Do I dare/Disturb the universe?/In a minute there is time/For decisions and revisions which a minute will reverse."

[33]G.K. Chesterton, *Orthodoxy* (Garden Ctiy: Image, 1924), pp. 39-40.

[34]Nabokov, *Lolita*, p. 167: Humbard desires to eat Lolita's lungs, liver, etc. A Zoroastrian myth describes the first parents who "loved" their children so much that they ate them. The gods then reduced human love by a factor of some 99 percent in order that future progeny would survive. Cf. Joseph Campbell, *Myths to Live By* (New York: Viking, 1972), pp. 153-54.

[35]Stern, "Death within life."

[36]Jennifer Jackson, "Virtue with Reason," *Philosophy*, vol. 53, no. 204 (1978), p. 229: We want to know "why we are 'bound' because man wants to know whether his sacrifice has been foolish."

[37]Chesterton, *Orthodoxy*, pp. 57-58.

[38]José Ortega y Gasset, *Obras completas* (Madrid: Revista de Occidente, 1965), 8:44: "Man is the being condemned to translate necessity into freedom." Cf. also *The Revolt of the Masses* (New York: Norton, 1932), p. 79: "Destiny does not consist in what we should like to do; rather it is recognized in its clear features in the consciousness that we must do what we do not feel like doing."

[39]Cf. Martin Buber, *I and Thou* (New York: Scribner, 1957), p. 59: "The free man is he who wills without arbitrary self-will. . . . He must sacrifice his puny, unfree will, that is controlled by things and instincts, to his grand will, which quits defined for destined being."

[40]"Alle Lust will Ewigkeit, will tiefe, tiefe Ewigkeit."

[41]Benedetto Croce, as quoted in Frankl, *The Failure of the Sexual Revolution*, p. 104.

[42]James Collins, *The Existentialists* (Chicago: Regnery, 1963), p. 167.

[43]Berdyaev, *The Death of Man*, pp. 239-40.

[44]Gabriel Marcel. "Obedience and Fidelity," *Homo Viatar* (New York: Harper Torchbooks, 1951), p. 134.

[45]Consider T.S. Eliot's exquisite phrase: "Distracted from distraction by distraction," *Four Quartets*, sec. III 'Burnt Norton'': "Only a flicker/Over the strained time-ridden faces/Distracted from distraction by distraction/Filled with fancies and empty of meaning/Tumid apathy with no concentration/Men and bits of paper, whirled by the cold wind."

[46]Stern, "Death within Life," p. 144.

[47]Mark 8:35: "For he who would save his life will love it: but he who loses his life for my sake and for the gospel's sake will save it. For what does it profit a man, if he gain the whole world, but suffer the loss of his own soul?"

[48]John 15:5.

[49]John 3:21.

13.
Morality and the Abandonment of Guilt

> At three I had a feeling of
>   Ambivalence toward my brothers.
> And so it follows naturally
>   I poisoned all my lovers.
> But now I'm happy; I have learned
>   The lesson this has taught;
> That everything I do that's wrong
>   Is someone else's fault.

—Anna Russell

Since the modern scientific world began in the sixteenth century, it is a strange and startling fact, as Chesterton notes, that "nobody's system of philoophy has really corresponded to everybody's sense of reality."[1] Philosophy, however, has not come to be an irrelevancy, esoteric and powerless; on the contrary, its effect on the masses may have become more potent and pervasive than it ever was in pre-modern days when faith had greater stature. But contemporary philosophy has achieved a function that is largely negative, instructing the masses—through tempting aphorisms and seductive stratagems—in how to dodge and avoid life's harsher truths. Philosophy, then, has come to rival reality, offering, as it does, an abstract anodyne for every anguish and a deceiving dream for each distress.

When we try to understand the nature of human guilt, therefore, we are immediately struck by the reality gap that separates so many popular modern philosophies from the testimony of universal human experience.

Guilt, as psychiatrist Marc Oraison describes it, is "one of the most radical realities of man."[2] Yet man prevailing philosophies teach that guilt is basically fictional and can be eliminated once for all by a decisive act of the will. At the same time, other philosophies that fare equally well with the populace contend that not only guilt but the will itself is a fiction and can be eliminated through a proper scientific understanding of human behavior.

Common sense (the universal "sense of reality") takes a more spacious view and boldly asserts that "guilt" as well as "will' and "science" are all real. The philosophy that is compatible with common sense and willing to embrace the full range of known realities, therefore, is much more to be preferred than any of the current models that selects its favorite slice of reality, raises it to the level of omni-importance and then banishes all else to the realm of mythology. The typical modern philosopher has developed a fashionable myopia which allows him to see only what he or his audience want to see; the rest is either too painful to acknowledge or simply does not happen to fit conveniently into his field of specialization. Thus, the radical existentialist sees will and virtually nothing else, while the sociobiologist sees nothing other than the predictable interactions of material parts.

In the modern age's evasion of private guilt, these two antithetic notions of will have played an important supporting role. In one case, the will is thought to live below the plane of moral responsibility; while in the other, it is thought to be of such Promethean strength as to be above it. In either case, neither sin nor guilt is considered real. Yet these views have proved to be as unsatisfactory as they are popular. Each evasion of guilt seems to deepen man's anxiety, and each denial of his will elicits the admonition that the world will be ruined unless he rectifies his will and re-assumes an attitude of moral responsibility. Against the heroic view of will, the protest is raised that freedom should be used in serving the needs of others in a limiting context that is always and inescapably loving and responsible.

Paradoxically, then, the major movements that evade private guilt do so for contradictory reasons: because the will is presumed too weak and because it is presumed too strong. This anomaly is a compelling sign that the modern world has been extravagant in its evasion of private guilt. It is an equally compelling sign of the need for a more comprehensive philosophy, one that can integrate "guilt", "will", "science", "sin", "freedom", and "moral responsibility", within the same human being.

All guilt-evading movements believe that guilt must be evaded because it immobilizes an individual, thereby seriously diminishing his chances for self-fulfillment. This is an unrealistic belief, however, as human history and clinical experience can attest. Guilt is not an indelible stigma; there are ways in which it can be expiated or dispelled. Evasion is an evasion from reality. Far from freeing man for self-fulfillment, his evasion of guilt keeps him shackled to his fears and anxieties. Freedom and fulfillment (here understood in the sense of personal authenticity) are achieved only after one has first acknowledged and accepted his guilt.

On the side of the weakened will, the scientific-analytic approach to man that is found in strict Freudian analysis has historical roots in the radical dualism of Descartes. The Cartesian partition of man into soul and body inaugurated a tradition in which scientists studied him as a mere body, while theologians and philosophers were left to regard him as a disembodied spirit. Since all human ills, psychic or somatic, are expressed on the physical level and scientists have no direct access to the movements of the soul, the belief naturally arose among scientists that man is a mere mechanism, though one of extraordinary complexity. Freud, in keeping with the requirements of his scientific model, compared man with a system of "hydraulics" and likened the libido to an "electromagnetic" charge.[3] Concurrently, theology and philosophy, left with the "ghost" in the machine, began to appear more and more like disciplines without valid subject matter. Thus, Descarte's radical dualism led inevitably to an acute crisis between science on the one hand, and philosophy and religion on the other.

According to the classical Freudian position, the great mistake of the Victorians was to stress "will power" at the price of repressing the sexual impulse. Freud considered this a most improvident arrangement inasmuch as it could lead to neurotic affects such as depression, anxiety, and panic—something he referred to as the "return of the repressed". His revolutionary solution was to turn the tables and free the sexual impulse by discounting the value of the will. As a result, Freud assigned the will a new function, that of inhibiting or repressing. Thus weakened and reduced to a negative role, the will could no longer be regarded as a factor positive enough to produce guilt. "Guilt feelings" (rather than guilt) were now understood as the result of repressing sexual feelings in the face of social constrictions and external authority. The will, then, to use philosopher Paul Ricoeur's image, was crushed in the dialectic of the sexual impulse (libido) and outside authority (super-ego).

The Freudian concept of guilt, then, portrays guilt as a factor of neurosis and as something false, unrealistic, and crippling—the result of too strict a socialization of the individual. However, guilt is never the fault of the individual but rather of the society or the authority that produces guilt feelings in the individual. In other words, *guilt feelings* do not arise from *guilt*. An individual does not *feel* guilt because of anything he did but because of a desire to do what he did not do that was repressed.

Rather than focus on man as directing his affairs through reason and will, the Freudian position, as psychologist O. Hobart Mowrer puts it, champions "the rights of the body in opposition to a society and moral order which are presumed to be unduly harsh and arbitrary."[4] Making antagonists of the "rights" of the body and the mores of society leads logically to insoluble practical contradictions: An individual believes he has a "right" to have sex simply because that is his desire, whereas society maintains it has a right to regulate human conduct in the interest of the common good because that is its reason. Likewise, the "no fault" philosophy—that ranges from casualty insurance to marriage contracts—is a technique for freeing individuals from private guilt by directing blame toward conditions or structures: people do not fail marriage, for example, but marriage fails people ("*it* didn't work").

Freudian psychology falls victim to the Cartesian heritage by accepting the radical split between body and soul, and failing to provide any basis for their interaction. Consequently, the Freudians submerge the will, a major power of the soul, into body and assign it a strictly negative function as a repressive agent in the formation of a neurosis. In so doing, they remove guilt from any association with the self. Man is guiltless because he is will-less. This notion of the will as too impotent to allow man to be *for* anything has led to a contemporary human crisis of sufficiently serious and pervasive proportions to prompt psychiatrist Leslie Farber to state that in this failure of the will lies the central pathology of our time.[5]

In his novel, *Lancelot*, Walker Percy satirizes the currently widespread view that man may be sick but can never be sturdy enough to commit a genuinely evil act. "The mark of the age", his protagonist exclaims, "is that terrible things happen but there is no 'evil' involved. People are either crazy, miserable, or wonderful, so where does the 'evil' come in?"[6] We find a comparable critique of our present age in John Cheever's *Falconer*, which reflects a similar concern about modern man's apparent loss of a sense of sin.

Claude Chabrol's 1975 film, *Just Before Nightfall*, presents feeling guilty as a mere *faux pas*, like hiring the wrong decorator or serving an inappropriate wine for dinner. After all, as the film suggests, man is too weak and life is too confusing for a person to be genuinely guilty of wrongdoing. The main character murders his mistress who is also the wife of his best friend. When he discloses his misdeed, in turn, to his wife and the victim's widower, he is astonished to find how understanding and sympathetic they are. Francois, the widower, says to him: "No one is guilty of what happens in a nightmare."[7]

Canadian authoress Barbara Amiel criticizes social democracy for teaching "that nothing is your fault." She explains that the Swedish word *trygghet* "implies a kind of warm, embracing security that protects the individual from everything that might disturb, or frighten, or penetrate the womb of gentle equilibrium that he has come to expect. No Swedish politician can avoid promising the continuance of *trygghet* if he wishes to survive."[8]

On the other hand, with the Death-of-God movement, man suddenly inherited the over-burdensome task of being like God but without benefit of His grace. Nietzsche's notion of the superman with his "will to power" called for a new morality that would overcome the inhibiting effects of guilt by throwing them off through sheer willpower. "Life consists of self-over-coming," he writes. "I estimate the power of a will according to how much resistance, pain, and torture it endures and knows how to transform into its own advantage."[7] Man is guiltless, then, not because he is will-less, but because the power of his will is limitless.

Walter Kaufmann carries the Nietzschean notion of the heroic will into the current discussion of guilt. At the close of his book *Without Guilt and Justice* he re-writes the temptation scene in Genesis, making the serpent wisdom's mouthpiece: "Once upon a time God decided, but now that he is dead it is up to you to decide. It is up to you to leave behind guilt and fear. You can be autonomous.''[10]

For Kaufmann, guilt is as unreal as it is for the Freudians. However, he enlists the power of the will to discharge guilt, whereas the Freudians see the negativity of the will as its cause. Like Nietzsche, Kaufmann emphasizes assertiveness, self-realization. Guilt is the effect of being submissive to another and is, therefore, an obstacle in the attainment of creative autonomy. Kaufmann advocates alienation[11] and discipline so that the self can be free to create. The Freudians advocate just the opposite so that man can function as an unimpeded mechanism. In both cases, when guilt is evaded, some other crucial factor is evaded in the process. When the "will to power" advocates evade guilt, they evade man's responsibilities to his neighbors (and to God); when the Freudians do, they evade man's capacity to function as a self. In either case there is a failure to achieve a balance between body and soul, self and other, creativity and morality.

The idea that man can throw off guilt by a mere effort of the will enjoys widespread popularity at the moment. Paula and Dick McDonald's *Guilt-Free*,[12] although it does not pretend in the least to be a serious work, presents guilt as simply a petty nuisance that we should be "above". Dr. Wayne Dyer's best seller *Your Erroneous Zones*[13] takes the equally simplistic position that guilt is useless and that no intelligent person will have anything to do with it. In widely circulated works of this like, readers are presented with a promise that is grounded in an unexamined contradiction, namely, that they will get along much better with others if they would only adopt a position of alienation which insulates them against being affected by others.

In the critically acclaimed movie *An Unmarried Woman*, the central character of the film goes to a professional therapist when her marriage of sixteen years comes to an end. The therapist enjoins her to get rid of all guilt. "Guilt", she explains, "is a man-made emotion" which one must "turn off." "And don't feel guilty about not feeling guilty," she warns, in a gentle but self-assured tone of voice. The scene is a paradigm for today's Hollywood concept of guilt. The contradictory nature of the advice is readily apparent. When a person is tormented by guilt, the thing he wants to do more than anything else in the world is to "turn it off". But this is precisely what he cannot do. The 'advice' is not really advice at all but merely a reiteration of exactly what it is that the client cannot do which brought her to seek the therapist in the first place. Secondly, if man's will is too ineffective to choose wrongs which register real guilt, then it can hardly be strong enough to banish guilt feelings in an instant.

Popular writers and film-makers on guilt naturally refrain from delineating the darker aspects of what their philosophies imply. Although their thinking may imply the need for attitudes of stoic alienation and Spartan willpower, they politely abstain from such unpleasant elucidations.

Kaufmann's book, on the other hand, is a serious treatment of guilt and written for a more discriminating audience. Thus, he is willing to announce that his position on eradicating guilt requires the eradication of justice and the adoption of alienation (including the overthrow of the Golden Rule). This kind of intellectual candor is most helpful in appraising secular attitudes toward guilt with those that are Christian. Bernard Häring, for example, states that alienation is the very essence of sin.[14]

Adherents of the Freudian or Nietzschean positions on guilt, although they ignore real private guilt, often attach guilt to large groups of people. Thus, they accuse the Church, capitalist governments, big corporations, or entire cultures of being guilty of wrongdoing, while exempting themselves from the same accusation. Such a view of guilt can produce an unnecessarily hostile and dangerous antagonism between the masses and the established order. It also can produce a self-defeating rejection of tradition.

Throughout history, in both literate and non-literate societies, the prevailing consensus has been that guilt is a natural, human response to one's complicity in wrongdong, and that man persists in suffering both in body and in soul when his guilt remains unconfessed and unatoned. The fact that it is commonplace, even fashionable, in today's society to regard private guilt as something false and therefore evadable, is owed largely to an avoidance of the critical distinction between true, objective guilt and the kind that is false and subjective. Throughout Kaufmann's extensive treatment of guilt, for exmple, nowhere does he make this distinction. Similarly, for Freud, all guilt is assumed to be abnormal.

There is no question that the determination of true or false guilt, both for the clinician as well as the individual himself, can be extremely problematic. However, this difficulty is rooted in the limitations of our knowledge of individual guilt in the particular case and not in the universal nature of guilt. Criteria exist which have proven most helpful in distinguishing true from false guilt in the majority of cases.

Psychiatrist Karl Stern offers four ways of separating "guilt" (true or objective guilt) from "neurotic guilt":[15] First, guilt has something in common with justice in that a proportion exists between the extent or grievousness of the wrongdoing and the degree or intensity of the guilt. In this respect, the French psychoanalyst Allendy had previously spoken of an "inner tribunal" or *justice intérieure*.[16] In neurotic guilt there exists no such proportion; a seemingly insignificant transgression can give rise to a prolonged and unbearable *feeling* of guilt. Secondly, guilt is something that can be paid or expiated (in several languages, the words for guilt and debt are synonymous). Neurotic guilt is insatiable. Next, objective guilt does not necessarily depend on emotion; an individual can recognize his wrongdoing and acknowledge it with calm. Neurotic guilt is inextricably interwoven with anxiety. Finally, guilt is related only to realized acts, while neurotic guilt is related to repressed drives as much as to realized acts.

Charles Odier, in 1943, had made the distinction between "functional guilt" (roughly equivalent to false guilt) and "value guilt" (true guilt), and drew up tables as a guide to the clear diagnosis of these distinct phenomena.[17] According to Odier, "functional guilt" is the result of social constraints, fear of taboos, or of losing the love of others. "Value guilt" is the consciousness of the self having betrayed an authentic standard; it is a free judgment of the self by the self.

More recently Paul Tournier has distinguished true from false guilt in terms of the former having its source ultimately in an opposition to God, while the latter originates in an opposition to the laws and suggestions of men.[18] Tournier notes that the actions for which we are reproached by God in our inner most hearts are usually very different from the acts for which we are reproached by men. He also presents in capsule form how other important thinkers distinguish guilt. Martin Buber differentiates "genuine" guilt from "neurotic" or "unreal" guilt by emphasizing that the former always turns on some violation of human relationships—a deliberate rupture of the I-Thou bond. Carl Jung views true guilt as stemming from a refusal of the self to integrate into consciousness the unpleasing parts of itself which he calls the "shadow." For Adler, the sense of guilt arises from a refusal to accept one's inferiority.[19] Each of these three forms of guilt may also be understood as being against the Will of God: A refusal to be whole, in the Jungian School, is tantamount to a refusal to be what God wants one to be; violation of relationships with others, for Buber, is equivalent to countermanding God's exhortation to love one's neighbor; not accepting one's inferiority, according to Adler's view is comparable to not accepting one's reality as a finite and defectible creature.

All thought that describes human behavior is based on the recognition that human existence is the dialectical focus of very broad but fundamental opposites. We speak of freedom and necessity, sanity and insanity, love and hate, normal and abnormal, conscious and unconscious, life and death. Such realities as these allow us to see man in a general way as the complex, ambivalent, multi-dimensional being he is. The distinction between true and false guilt is rooted in and consistent with these more fundamental opposites. There is no reason to believe that guilt is the great mono-dimensional exception in man's existence. The overwhelming evidence is that the recognition, acceptance, and expiation of real guilt allows man to evolve on the side of freedom, sanity, love, normality, consciousness, and life; whereas its evasion inclines him to all the contrary opposites. Mowrer concludes that "increasingly it appears that the central fact in personality disorder is *real* guilt and that it can be radically resolved only by confession that has at least a quasi-public character."[20]

Karl Stern remarks that in his experience the question concerning the difference between real (objective) and neurotic guilt is the one that comes up with the greatest frequency.[23] Although the difference between the two has been amply elaborated and has proved its usefulness on the personal and clinical levels, the popular tendency to lump all guilt into one kind—neurotic guilt—has persisted. This undiscerning approach to the problem of guilt has been a boon to the therapist and a bane to the moralist and religious counsellor. For, if all guilt is neurotic, then its presence in an individual must be symptomatic of sickness. This theory of uniform guilt has led to an excessive preoccupation with trying to gain *insight* into *why* an individual experiences guilt feelings by probing his unconscious. Mowrer remarks flatly that secular psychotherapy "does not really believe in guilt, only guilt feelings,"[22] and criticizes it for its exclusive concentration on such *insight* to the absolute neglect of repentance and restitution. He goes on to quote a distinguished seminary professor who makes the searing comment that "in so far as Christians have fallen for the notion that guilt is a sickness they have made theological donkeys of themselves."[23]

A few decades ago, Dietrich Bonhoeffer observed that many Christian churches were preaching a new form of salvation that avoided the personal "embarrassment" of confession; he condemned this teaching as "the doctrine of cheap grace."[24] Bonhoeffer argued that making grace available at so low a cost was equivalent to a kind of magician's Christianity that justifies the wrongdoing without justifying the wrongdoer. In this view, guilt is not considered real enough to involve the Christian or his church in any formal way.

Guilt is as real as the will is functional; and the will is functional to the extent that human actions are not pre-determined. Alongside those who have labored to define guilt as sickness, a group of socio-biologists has emerged that effectively dismissed guilt by insisting that freedom is an illusion we must go beyond. Yet, who can heed such an invitation but one who is already free? These behaviorists are trapped by the logic of their own first premise. Harvard's Edward Wilson, for example, author of a mammoth 700-page book, *Sociobiology: The New Synthesis*, calls for "ethics to be removed temporarily from the hands of the philosophers and biologicized."[25] But if all human behavior is pre-determined, making such a request—in fact, any request at all—contradicts behaviorism's basic principle that everything is pre-determined. The all too patent contradiction between what these scientists report and how eagerly they promote it seems to defeat their own thesis. If socio-biologism truly reflects the human condition, then no one is free either to accept or reject it. It would seem that its promoters urge its acceptance upon non-believers only because they really do not believe it themselves.

The various attempts to evade real guilt either directly by treating it as a sickness or indirectly by denying freedom have either contradicted personal, clinical, and historical experience or have contradicted logic itself. Nonetheless, the effort to evade guilt persists. This phenomenon may best be understood as the result of a desire to avoid the pain and disgrace that are associated with an honest recognition of oneself and the implications of one's deeds—as the result, therefore, of a desire for moral anesthesia.

Apathy is a defense against pain—in the case of real guilt, the pain that accompanies the awareness of one's complicity in evil—that is achieved through a withdrawal of love and will.[26] It is, as Harry Stack Sullivan states, "a miracle of protection by which a personality in utter fiasco rests until it can do something else."[27] Apathy assumes the attitude of "I don't care," "it doesn't matter," or "nothing can be done, anyway." Thus, it joins hands with cynicism to form a fortress against moral involvement in the real world. It describes the ultimate tragic condition of man when, by protecting him from all awareness of the tragic, it inevitably, though unintentionally, begins to deprive him of all awareness of the good. Consequently, apathy, rather than hate, is the true opposite of love. An individual cannot endure the dumb, cold, feelingless state of apathy indefinitely, for it contradicts everything about his essential nature as a loving and willing being. Inexorably, apathy leads to impotence, addiction, and self-destructive hostility. Karl Menninger proposes that the only practical antidote for today's pandemic moral malaise is a "deliberate renunciation of apathy and a courageous facing of the responsibility for evil."[28]

Denial is another common way of evading the pain of guilt. In one classic form of guilt-denial, the individual assumes the mask of moral innocence, a comportment Rollo May describes as "pseudo-innocence."[29] Here, the individual denies complicity in wrongdoing, preferring to take refuge in a delusional world of innocence, rather than deal with the pain or disgrace that might accompany the honest admission of his actions. The denial mechanism is rich in reassurance but poor in realism, for, as playwright Arthur Miller expounds, it is "more reassuring to see the world in terms of totally innocent victims and totally evil instigators of the monstrous violence we see all about."[30] Denial, paradoxically, is the will caught in the impossible task of trying to efface its own act. Denial, then, like apathy, leads away from reality and away from one's self-acceptance as a totality that includes the dimensions of love, will, and moral responsibility. Denial is akin to the "Who me?" attitude of the fearful and immature child who is not yet ready to accept the full burden of the consequences of his acts.

Repression, another mechanism that can be enlisted in the service of guilt-evasion, consists in submerging the disturbing reality of one's wrongdoing into the unconscious. In this case, the individual is freed, at least temporarily, from the conscious realization of what he has repressed, although his guilt, existing below the level of his awareness, is still part of him. Mowrer has taken the original Freudian notion of repression, which is a repression of *impulse* arising from the *id*, and given it new co-ordinates. Accordingly, repression is a repression of *guilt* arising from one's *conscious acts*.[31] In other words, Mowrer exchanges Freud's "impulse theory" of neurosis for his own "guilt theory". Thus, the counter-productive character of guilt-repression becomes evident: the individual represses guilt in order to spare himself pain, but in so doing lays the groundwork for a potential neurosis. Repression, then, like apathy and denial, does not really protect the individual from guilt but only offers an illusion of protection. What it does achieve, in effect, is to mask guilt, thereby making it more difficult for the individual to come to terms with both himself and the real consequences of his acts.

Projection, in the case of guilt, is the transferring of an individual's own guilt to another or to a group of others, all of whom are usually innocent of the evil at issue. A striking historical example of guilt-projection is found in the records of the Nuremburg trials. Rosenberg and Streicher, the philosophers and publicists of the Nazi movement, disclaimed any responsibility for the slaughter of 2.5 million Jews at Auschwitz because they did not believe their ideas would have led to such an action. At the same time, Colonel Hoess, the officer in charge of the mass murders at Auschwitz, blamed the philosophers and publicists for his believing that the Jews were to blame for everything, and deserved extermination. Here we see the Nazis projecting their guilt onto the Jews, the philosophers and publicists blaming the executioners, and the executioners themselves blaming the philosophers and publicists.[32] In projection, it is not enough that the guilty individual be regarded as innocent; someone else must be charged with his guilt. Consequently, projection, like apathy, establishes a pre-disposition to violence. Like all the other mechanisms for evading guilt, it represents a movement away from reality, self, will, freedom, consciousness and love.

In addition to the pain and disgrace that are associated with an admission of one's guilt is the fearful sense of death. St. Paul's well known phrase that "the wages of sin is death" (Romans 6:23) alludes to the immanence of death in the experience of guilt. Every experience of guilt must be an experience of death since guilt implies our free choice not to fulfill our destiny, not to be what we were meant to be.

Paul Tillich describes guilt as the anxiety of death we experience when non-being threatens our moral self-affirmation.[33] Guilt reminds us of death because we fear that unexpiated guilt must lead to condemnation, or eternal death in a moral sense. The unrealistic strategy that is fashionable today is to believe that if there is no sin there can be no guilt and consequently no moral death. But this strategy, if carried out, must lead to a crippling neurosis. For if there is no guilt there is no moral freedom and therefore man cannot, in principle, choose his proper destiny; he is therefore condemned never to be the moral being he was meant to be. Man must acknowledge guilt in order to acknowledge his freedom and recongize that he is required to answer for what he makes of himself. People evade guilt, then, because they believe, unrealistically, that this is one way they can cheat death. Yet by evading guilt they evade life—their life as free, accountable moral beings.

However painful and unsettling the acceptance of private guilt may promise to be, it does not begin to compare, in potential pain and dissolution, with what is augured by these desperate attempts to evade it. In her introduction to the *Time* edition of C.S. Lewis' immortal *Screwtape Letters*, Phyllis McGinley states that "of all losses man has sustained in the past hundred years, no deprivation has been so terrible as the abandonment of private guilt."[34] It was more dreadful than losing his Creator, McGinley argues, because, in substituting shame for sin, society amputated half of the human psyche, thereby making man ineligible for either wholeness or forgiveness. Thus weakened and deprived of hope, "guiltless" man suffers more acutely the very death he seeks to evade. Mowrer concurs. "To have the excuse of being 'sick' rather than sinful," he reasons, "is to court the danger of also becoming lost. . . . In becoming amoral, ethically neutral, and 'free', we have cut the very roots of our being; lost our deepest sense of self-hood and identity; and with neurotics themselves, find ourselves asking: 'who am I?' "[35]

Guilt has the disconcerting—one might even call it "diabolical"— property of tightening its hold on man the more he tries to evade it. In fact, one cannot evade guilt, but only banish it to a deeper region of the psyche where it is more difficult to dispel and where it can do more harm. Acknowledged guilt which is confessed, is dispelled with relative ease. But guilt that is submerged into the unconscious may fester and form a neurosis which presents a problem of a much more complicated nature. Modern counsellors applaud Ricoeur's suggestion that neurosis be regarded as "a failure to exonerate oneself of guilt."[36]

Psychotherapists report a current shifting of guilt which finds people struggling not so much with moral problems per se, but with the more abstruse problem of their psychological responses to their moral decisions. A woman who chooses not to be party to a premarital adventure may be anxious about whether her decision is symptomatic of "morbid repression." On the other hand, if she agrees to the affair, she may worry about her ability to perform and question whether she is sufficiently "liberated". According to popular literature, the question men ask is no longer "Will she or won't she?" but "Can she or can't she?" This type of shift is comparable to the change from an ethos that repressed instinct to protect conscience to the kind of "new morality" that represses conscience in order to free instinct.

Such a shifting of guilt, which only makes guilt a more diffuse and complicated problem, well illustrates its insuppressible character. But it also bears a serious *caveat*. Shifting concern away from conscience and moral actions to an uncensored release of libidinal energy is tantamount to a repression of conscience. Conscience is a product of consciousness. It operates under the light of reason and aids in controlling one's moral actions against the indiscriminate urgings of instinct. Repression of conscience, therefore, is regressive because it surrenders the powers of discretion to primitive, archaic impulses that are incapable of discretion. (If ever the word "archaic" had a pejorative connotation, it is as used here.) This psychic realm of primitive instinct, as psychotherapists inform us, literally "pulsates with anxiety" and harbors the irrational seeds of our potential self-destruction.[37]

Mowrer maintains that Freud never fully apprehended the essential nature of anxiety. For Freud, anxiety comes from the repression of acts which the individual did not dare commit. Mowrer parts company with Freud, having found what he regards as decisive evidence for his own thesis—that anxiety arises from a repression of the acts which the individual did commit but wishes he had not.[38] For Freud, anxiety is caused by false guilt; for Mowrer (and others), real guilt causes anxiety.

We find a dramatic illustration of the repressing and deadening of conscience that can cause anxiety in an exmaple used by C.F. Bajema in his book *Abortion and the Meaning of Personhood*. The author refers to a woman who underwent a suction abortion and was invited by her doctor to view the fetal remains in a jar. The woman reported that she "felt nothing" upon viewing the dismembered body of her unborn child. But what she did confess to feeling was her troubling *absence* of guilt and her *fright* because her own numb conscience made her feel "one" with the "butchers at Buchenwald" who could view heaps of dead bodies in mass graves with calm and not "feel a thing."[39]

In a different way, attempts to evade guilt can cause guilt to affect other areas of one's conscious life. An individual commits adultery, let us say, and experiences consequent guilt. But he eschews the sacraments, preferring to stay with his mistress. He then feels guilty about his abandoning his religion. Here, guilt is added to guilt, the operative principle being that if guilt is not dispelled it is dispersed.

A final illustration of the insuppressible character of guilt appears in a *Time* magazine citation which describes the psychology of the typical citizen of modernity who "flagellates himself equally for his marginal failures at orgasm and for his secret indifference to minorities, for badly relating to his children and for not relating at all to children in Pakistan. He has chucked sin, but taken on cosmic guilt, including the ultimate guilt—feeling guilty about not feeling guilty."[40]

The Freudian theory of guilt as sickness may very well be a direct outgrowth of the Nietzschean position that guilt is a weakness. Nietzsche saw no value in guilt because God—and with Him, objective moral standards—was dead. Freud, as a psychoanalyst, could not abolish guilt so easily, but he reduced its presence in the individual to a neurosis by denying the human will its positive character. Thus, God was dead and man was broken. However, something akin to what Freud himself recognized as the "return of the repressed" was to have its day of triumph. The guilt which was thought abolished returned with greater vengeance: the Freudians began to feel guilty that they had never lived; the Nietzscheans, because they had never cared.

Dostoevsky's character in *Crime and Punishment*, Raskolnikov, conducts an experiment in murder to test his thesis that he is an exceptional individual and therefore above the moral order. The test backfires and Raskolnikov is haunted by guilt. He is unable to restore order to his life until he confesses and atones for his crime. In a more recent celebrated novel, *The Stranger*, Camus' Nietzschean character, Raymond, commits a senseless murder and feels no remorse whatsoever. In fact, although he is sentenced to death for his crime, it scarcely occurs to him to feel regret. What occupies his mind during the trial is his belief that he is morally superior to the hypocrites who condemn him because he refused to cry at his mother's funeral.

Dostoevsky's novel deals with real guilt, objective moral standards, and the notion that unconfessed guilt is an obstacle to personal wholeness and authenticity. Camus' novel deals with false guilt (that the crowd was trying to impose on Raymond), the non-existence of objective moral standards, and the notion that will is stronger than moral law (which implies the correlative notion that private guilt is an absurdity).

Is the philosophy of Camus a sign of the times? It very well may be, for the current ethos puts great stock in the notion that guilt is fictional and objective morality an impediment to growth. We find this thought reflected in a wide variety of philosophies and fashions ranging from atheistic existentialism to Freudian psychoanalysis and sociobiology; from "pop" therapy to current fads as well as contemporary literature and films. Yet, all these views, divergent as they are, neglect two areas of critical importance: The first has to do with the criteria by which the reality of guilt is distinguished from guilt that is unreal, false, imposed, or neurotic; the second has to do with the fact that just as libidinal desires can be repressed, so too can conscience, the "inner tribunal" and conscious arbiter of good and evil, be repressed. The current ethos has not absolved man of private guilt; it simply has confused real guilt with unreal guilt, and the repression of conscience with the repression of desire.

Citizens of the modern era have made a concerted effort to evade guilt, as if they fully expected that the great promises of progress that technology provided would free them not only from the burden of labor but also from the pain of guilt. The mechanisms of apathy, denial, repression, and projection were employed as an anesthetic would be applied to a painful wound. However, these mechanisms proved to be counter-productive, leading inevitably not only to more pain but also to self-alienation, regression, neurotic behavior, and even violence. The anesthetic that was used initially to deaden a dull pain led to the use of the analgesic designed to relieve a sharper one; all along, however, what was most needed was an analeptic to increase awareness, painful or not, of what was really happening.

It belongs to the nature of real guilt to possess an individual more, the more he tries to evade it. This fact demonstrates both the real character of guilt and the truth that man cannot conquer guilt either through will-power, therapy, or any of the sundry evasion techniques that he has at his disposal. Only through acceptance, confession, and atonement can an individual dispel real guilt and resume his growth as an integrated and authentic person who lives and interacts with others. And only a philosophy that accepts things because they are true—rather than because they are pleasing, or ego-gratifying, or fashionably scientific—can really correspond to everybody's "sense of reality."

NOTES

[1]Gilbert Keith Chesterton, *Saint Thomas Aquinas, The Dumb Ox* (Garden City: Doubleday, 1956), p. 145.

[2]Marc Oraison, "Psychology and the Sense of Sin", in *Sin*, trans. B. Murchland and R. Meyerpeter (N.Y.: Macmillan, 1962), p. 27.

[3]See Rollo May, *Love and Will* (N.Y.: Norton, 1969), p. 208.

[4]O. Hobart Mowrer, *The Crisis in Psychiatry and Religion* (Princeton, N.J.: Van Nostrand, 1961) p. 82.

[5]Leslie Farber, *The Ways of the Will* (N.Y.: Basic Books, 1965).

[6]Walker Percy, *Lancelot* (N.Y.: Farrar, Straus & Giroux, 1977), p. 139.

[7]See the review by Jay Cocks, *Time*, Sept. 29, 1975, p. 48.

[8]Barbara Amiel, *Confessions* (Toronto: Macmillan of Canada, 1980), p. 125.

[9]Walter Kaufmann, *Nietzsche: Philosopher, Psychologist, Antichrist* (Princeton: Princeton University Press, 1950), p. 183.

[10]Walter Kaufmann, *Without Guilt and Justice* (N.Y.: Peter Wyden, 1973), p. 236.

[11]Kaufmann, *Without Guilt*, "But any claim that we need alienation does not depend on a marginal use of the term. What I mean is the condition of feeling estranged—above all, from one's fellow men, but also from the universe, and from oneself. I shall argue that alienation is the price of self-consciousness, autonomy, and integrity." p. 140.

[12]Paula and Dick McDonald, *Guilt-Free* (N.Y.: Grosset and Dunlap, 1977).

[13]Wayne Dyer, *Your Erroneous Zones* (N.Y.: Funk and Wagnalls, 1976). "Guilt is the most useless of all erroneous zone behaviors. It is by far the greatest waste of emotional energy. Why? Because, by definition, you are feeling immobilized in the present over something that has *already* taken place and no amount of guilt can ever change history." p. 91. Another work of the same ilk is: Manuel J. Smith, *When I Say No I Feel Guilty* (N.Y.: Bantam, 1975).

[14]Bernard Haering, C.Ss.R., *Sin in the Secular Age* (Garden City: Doubleday, 1974), Chapter 2.

[15]Karl Stern, *The Third Revolution* (N.Y.: Harcourt, Brace and Co., 1954), pp. 202-208.

[16]René Allendy, *Justice intérieure* (Paris: Denoél and Steele, 1931). Allendy's contributions here are of special significance to Christian counsellors because Allendy is a non-believer.

[17]Charles Odier, *Les deux sources, consciente et inconsciente de la vie morale* (Neuchâtel: LaBaconnière, 1943).

[18]Paul Tournier, *Guilt and Grace*, trans. A. Heathcote et al. (N.Y.: Harper and Row, 1962), pp. 63-71.

[19]Tournier, p. 65.

[20]Mowrer, p. 217.

[21]Karl Stern, "The Problem of Guilt," *Love and Success* (N.Y.: Farrar, Straus and Giroux, 1975), p. 64.

[22]Mowrer, p. 107.

[23]Mowrer, p. 170.

[24]Dietrich Bonhoeffer, *The Cost of Discipleship* (N.Y.: Macmillan, 1948). "Cheap grace means the justification of sin without the justification of the sinner." p. 35. "The price we are having to pay today in the shape of the collapse of the organized church is only the inevitable consequence of our policy of making grace available to all at too low a cost." p. 45.

[25]See "Why You Do What You Do, Sociobiology: A New Theory of Behavior," *Time*, August 1, 1977, pp. 36-41.

[26]Rollo May, p. 33. See also Rollo May, *Man's Search for Himself* (N.Y.: Norton, 1953). "Apathy and the lack of feeling are also defenses against anxiety." p.25.

[27]Harry Stack Sullivan, *The Psychiatric Interview* (N.Y.: Norton, 1954), p. 184.

[28]Karl Menninger, *Whatever Became of Sin?* (N.Y.: Hawthorne, 1973), p. 189.

[29]Rollo May, *Power and Innocence* (N.Y.: Norton, 1972), p. 49. See J.A. Johnston and D. B. Roberts, *Catholic Women and Abortion: A Profile, Sample and Case Study* (Sidney, Australia: Rigney House, 1978). A woman who willingly underwent an abortion denied her compliance in the act in these words: "What happens under an anesthetic is out of my control . . . and has nothing to do with my decision making." pp. 109-110.

[30]May, *Power*, p. 47.

[31]Mowrer, pp. 26ff.

[32]See Gordon Allport, *The Nature of Prejudice* (Garden City: Doubleday, 1954), p. 56. See also Tournier, "The majority of Roman Catholics who criticize their Church discover, when they have been helped to become entirely sincere with themselves, that their criticisms are a screen for a feeling of guilt at having avoided confession." p. 151.

[33]Paul Tillich, *The Courage to Be* (New Haven: Yale University Press, 1965), p. 41.

[34]Phyllis McGinley in the Introduction to C.S. Lewis, *Screwtape Letters* (N.Y.: Time, 1963), p. xviii.

[35]O. Hobart Mowrer, "Sin, the Lesser of Two Evils" in *American Psychologist*, XV (1960), 301-304.

[36]Tournier, p. 136.

[37]See Stern, *Revolution*, pp. 203-4.

[38]O. Hobart Mowrer, "Anxiety Theory as a Basis for Distinguishing between Counselling and Psychotherapy," *Concepts and Programs of Counselling, ed. R.F. Berdie (Minneapolis: University of Minnesota Press, 1953)*.

[39]Clifford E. Bajema, *Abortion and the Meaning of Personhood* (Grand Rapids, Michigan: Baker Book House, 1974), p. 72. See also M.J. Sobran, "Six Years After," *The Human Life Review*, J.P. McFadden ed. Vol. V, No. 1, 1979 (Winter), p. 11: "Anesthetizing the conscience seems to be an essential part of the abortion 'procedure'."

[40]Quoted in Bp. Fulton J. Sheen, *Those Mysterious Priests* (Garden City: Doubleday, 1974), p. 240.

Index

Members of the Christendom Publishing Group, continued.

Mr. Nicholas J. Mulhall
Mr. Joseph F. O'Brien
Mr. Lawrence P. O'Shaughnessy
Mrs. Veronica M. Oravec
Robert N. Pelaez, M.D.
Mr. & Mrs. Joseph and Mary Peek
Mr. & Mrs. William H. Power, Jr.
Rev. T. A. Rattler, O.S.A.
Rev. Robert A. Reed
Mrs. John F. Reid
Dr. Charles E. Rice
Bro. Philip Romano, O.F.M. Cap.
Mr. Richard W. Sassman
Mrs. Marian C. Schatzman
Miss Constance M. Scheetz
Mrs. Margaret Scheetz
Mrs. Clargene Schmidt
Mr. & Mrs. Ralph Schutzman
Mr. Frank P. Scrivener
Dr. John B. Shea

Mr. W. R. Sherwin
Mrs. Walter Skorupski
Mrs. Mary Smerski
Mr. Vincent C. Smith
Mrs. William Smith
Mrs. Ann Spalding
Mr. Edward S. Szymanski
Mr. Raymond F. Tesi
Rev. Frederick J. Vaughn
Mr. William C. Vinet, Jr.
Rev. George T. Voiland
Mr. & Mrs. David and Marie Walkey
Honorable Vernon A. Walters
Mr. Fulton John Waterloo
Mr. Ralph A. Wellings
Mr. John R. Wilhelmy
Mrs. Mary Williams
Mr. Michael C. Winn
James F. Zimmer, M.D.